UNLOCK THE GIANT WITHIN

UNLOCK THE GIANT WITHIN

DAVID PILLING

authorHOUSE®

AuthorHouse™
1663 Liberty Drive
Bloomington, IN 47403
www.authorhouse.com
Phone: 1-800-839-8640

First published by AuthorHouse   07/01/2011

ISBN: 978-1-4567-8676-2 (sc)
ISBN: 978-1-4567-8677-9 (ebk)

Printed in the United States of America

Any people depicted in stock imagery provided by Thinkstock are models, and such images are being used for illustrative purposes only.
Certain stock imagery © *Thinkstock.*

This book is printed on acid-free paper.

CONTENTS

INTRODUCTION

Within themselves, everybody in the world contains the seeds of greatness—no matter how modest that greatness may be. However, their potential often remains untapped. Why is this so?

People do not often realise and appreciate the immense capacity for achievement within each of us. Those who achieve greatness do so because they are prepared to tread where no person has trod before. More importantly, there something inside that drives them to achieve what they want to achieve. I am not suggesting you must become a world leader, but I believe we can all do better and, in doing so, achieve greater satisfaction from life. But understand this: the choice is entirely yours. It is not for me to suggest what you must or must not do. If you want more, you can achieve your life's ambitions.

Success is in the eye of the beholder. 'Advancement' may mean something entirely different to me than it does to you, but I believe it means becoming better than we are now.

In the short history of humankind, there has never been a better time to do so. Today, many people from ordinary backgrounds achieve a status once thought not to be possible. A film star became one of the most powerful men in the world and a lawyer from South Africa became a humanitarian inspiration to millions. We may not all become world leaders but we can achieve the success and status we desire. Others have done it—why not you?

If you wish to be a follower instead of a leader, that is entirely your right. If that is the role you choose, don't be envious of those who show leadership.

However, the simple fact is that most people desire advancement into leadership in some way or another, whether large or small.

It is important to remember that you do not have to be a great leader to feel fulfilled. Any mother or father with a natural urge to love and cherish their child can feel a sense of fulfillment unmatched by any other accomplishment. You do not have to achieve greatness to feel fulfilled; each step forward you take in your life will give you a level of fulfillment.

At the end of the day, we must each make our own choice. If this choice is made consciously, there is no right or wrong. We all have a giant within us with the capacity to do anything we desire. Once you make your choice, you too can reach inside yourself and 'Unlock the Giant Within'.

CHAPTER I

IN THE BEGINNING

It is easy to forget that the world was not always like it is today. In the early days of civilisation, the world transcended from an age of tribal leaders to a new age of kings. There was no democracy; these kings handed down their authority to their family successors, whether or not they were qualified for the task. Very few of these leaders were truly great. For example, English royalty can trace their lineage back almost 2,000 years, yet in that time few of these leaders achieved greatness. Indeed, thanks to the detailed recorded history of these kings and queens, we know the greater majority of them were not qualified to lead a nation.

Of course, there are exceptions to this rule of hereditary leadership, the most notable being Alexander the Great, who, from the age of eighteen, led an army that conquered most of the known world. This example proves that greatness is not a state into which one is born, but something that must be achieved regardless of hereditary lineage. True leadership has been shown by men who did not inherit it, including Julius Caesar, Jesus Christ, Mohammad[1], Genghis Khan and many others.

Throughout the ages, people at the bottom of the stack, such as slaves and serfs, were totally controlled throughout their lives by the so-called nobility and forced to obey their masters' every whim. The seeds of democracy were planted in Ancient Rome, yet people envious of true leadership murdered Julius Caesar because he was a perceived threat to their way of life. This heralded a new age of hereditary rulers who dispensed evil, like Caligula and Nero.

---

[1]

The French Revolution, with its ideals of liberty and fraternity, eventually resulted in the reign of yet another dictator: Napoleon. However, the difference lay in that he was a true leader who rose from the rank of Corporal, just as Hitler did two centuries later.

Liberty did not truly dawn until the drafting of the American Declaration of Independence, which allowed free men to succeed through free enterprise. It took over a 100 years for Britain to reluctantly catch up with the Americans. Certainly, the Industrial Revolution did create a number of wealthy men at the expense of their workers. Whilst there had been a Parliament in London for several centuries, there was still no true democracy because not everyone had a vote.

World War 1 was caused by the ignorance and arrogance of the leaders of Austria, Germany and Russia. None of these monarchs were qualified to lead, particularly Tsar Nicholas II of Russia. Kaiser William of Germany was an arrogant monarch, drunk with power and exercising it for his own egotistical purposes. Germany's invasion of Belgium prompted Britain to honour a treaty and come to Belgium's aid, thus involving them in a catastrophic war.

At that time, a huge number of the army corps' officers had obtained their rank by buying their commission. This not only applied to junior officers but also to those in the senior ranks. At the first battle of the Somme, the flower of British youth was massacred as unqualified generals sent thousands of men to die in a hail of shellfire and machine gun bullets. The soldiers were instructed to walk into battle, just like the armies of Napoleon and Wellington at Waterloo one 100 years earlier. What is more, the same scene continued for four years, with millions of lives lost in appalling conditions simply to gain a few 100 metres of worthless soil.

Horrific though World War 2 was, the conflict featured many well-considered strategies and tactics, and huge gains. That was not the lot for the poor devils in World War 1. Prior to this catastrophe, the working class people in Britain worked in appalling conditions and it is hardly a wonder that there was a backlash via the growing power of the trade union movement which peaked decades later.

The political landscape began to transform during the twentieth century. One of the most significant changes was that ordinary men from humble backgrounds began to have a voice. Some of those voices, such as McDonald and Franklin D. Roosevelt, spoke only for only good, whilst others, like Lenin, Hitler and Stalin, acted more appallingly than the monarchies they had overthrown. Ordinary men, many from working class backgrounds, were able to rise to power on their own abilities.

Since the 1950s, opportunities have been created for all men and women to succeed. We no longer have to be born into success. Some of the wealthiest men in the world today started from virtually nothing. Now, success is available to all simply by reaching out and taking it. The most wonderful thing is that you do not have to achieve "greatness" to be great. All success is great, no matter how small or insignificant. It is relative.

In fact, there are three ways to succeed:

- On purpose—by planning
- By chance—by winning
- By theft—by stealing

The beauty of today's world is that we all have the potential to succeed. Of course, you do not have to succeed if you don't want to. It is a matter of choice, and if that is the way you choose you must be satisfied with the result. If, however, you wish to have more, you cannot point the finger at someone else. You can only point that finger at yourself.

Realise that you will never get it right all the time. If you go to the casino and win 51 per cent of the time, you are winning. If you go to university and get over 80 per cent on your exams, you graduate with Honours. You will not get it right every time, but when you foul up, as you undoubtedly will, you must recognise your mistakes and do something to correct them. Don't sit on your hands.

If you have ever wanted more than you already have, then start by "taking off your old jacket." What does this mean? Simply this: when you go to a store to buy a new suit, you select a style and colour you like in a size you think will fit you. Next, you go to the change room to try on the jacket and see if it will fit. If you try to put that jacket on over your old jacket, it will not fit. If you want a new jacket, you have to first take off the old one.

It took humanity nearly 10,000 years to develop the horse-drawn cart. Yet in following 100 years we put a man on the moon. Even greater than this achievement is the knowledge we have gained about the wonders of the universe to a point where we are close to reproducing the Big Bang.

It may not be everyone's desire to achieve what great men like Einstein or Stephen Hawking achieved, but it is important to realise that the only difference between them and us is a sense of self-belief and the knowledge that we can also achieve great things. Anyone can do it. It is not a matter of intelligence; it is a matter of will. We have all seen people with physical or intellectual disabilities achieve incredible things relative to their situation. If they can do it, then I ask, "Why not you?"

What does it mean to 'Unlock the Giant Within'? It simply means reaching inside oneself and unlocking the huge potential we all have to advance and better ourselves.

Let us first examine one of the more important qualities that we need.

1. EDUCATION

To receive an education is important. Understand, though, that the only thing it achieves is to qualify us for the job and bring us to the starting line.

Learning

As adults, our learning should already be advanced. Our formative years are from birth to the age of seven. Centuries ago, the Jesuits said, "Give me the child until he is seven and I will show you the man." Too much "education" and not enough learning can be very wasteful. I once knew a man from New Zealand who had spent years writing his Ph.D. thesis on an extinct indigenous tribe. That is education for education's sake. It is not learning.

No new discovery made in the world today has been taught before; it has been developed in the mind of its discoverer. This is the process of learning. Get an education by all means, but understand is it what you learn from there on that matters. During that process, do not allow yourself to "major on minors". In fact, be impatient with the things that bog you down.

Work this out if you can. All knowledge fits into three categories:

- You know what you know
- You know what you do not know
- You don't know what you don't know

Once you understand the last point, you will be able to begin the adventure of discovering yourself and realising the fullness of your potential.

Initiative

If you simply follow orders and do things others tell you to do, your personal growth will be at a snail's pace.

When Lawrence of Arabia was sent into the desert to "appreciate the situation", no one could have foreseen the enormity of what he would achieve by using his initiative. Lawrence placed no boundaries upon himself. He became a household name around the world, but people had to go to the Imperial War Museum to find out who his commander, General Allenby, was—and Allenby's achievements were also considerable. Why Lawrence allowed his life to disappear into obscurity, no one will ever know. Perhaps, after Unlocking the Giant Within, he felt he had fulfilled his ambition. In my view, he was entitled to do this.

In the armed forces, the golden rule—"follow your orders"—is insisted upon, but so is the idea that "an officer must use his initiative at all times." It seems a contradiction, doesn't it? But in the long practice and application of conflict, it has been found to hold true.

Understand that if you live a life of following orders, you will always be limited by what others will tell you to do. Initiative is a vital and necessary element of your personal growth.

Character

When General Schwarzkopf was asked for the most important quality he looked for in his officers, he answered, "Character." I must admit I find it difficult to readily explain what character consists of. It covers a seemingly endless range of qualities. One of those qualities is to be different, to stand out and demonstrate exceptional abilities. Another is to have a personality to which people are attracted. Yet another quality is strength, as most people wish to rely on someone. Another is leadership, in either a small or a large way. There are many other qualities of character.

Character is always developed. For example, many people are born with huge disadvantages. These could be economic, criminal or financial—the list goes on. If we allow ourselves to copy our environment, we demonstrate little character. If, however, we do not let a wealthy environment spoil us, or a poor environment limit us, we will develop character. We are all products of our environment, but it is those who change [despite?] their environment that possess character.

Empathy

This quality may not seem to fit with the other characteristics, especially when considered in terms of dictators such as Hitler, Stalin and Mao Zedong. In my wildest dreams, I could not possibly imagine people like these being elected leaders of the United States, Britain, Germany or even Russia and China. However, throughout the twentieth century, particularly since World War 2, the world has changed. Since the horrors of the two world wars, the attitude of the world's population has altered. Whilst wars still continue, the mass killings, horror and atrocities have diminished to the unusual and remote. Further evidence of this change has been demonstrated recently in areas of the Middle East, where populations refuse to be held under a dictatorship and the people demand democracy.

There was a huge change in attitude by victorious nations when we compare the end of World War 1 to the end of World War 2. The Treaty of Versailles, engineered by the French to seek reparation and revenge from Germany, was the root cause of World War 2. If it were not for the Treaty of Versailles, Hitler would not have had a platform from which to launch his fanaticism. Compare this with the Marshall Plan after World War 2, where the victors—particularly the United States—saw it as a priority to fund the defeated powers of Germany and Japan by providing billions for their restructure.

There has also been change at the grass roots of society. Workers' rights were enforced almost to the point of self-destruction, especially in Britain, where a balance was finally formed to ensure executives could no longer exploit workers. Today's most successful people have learned to work with their colleagues, whether they are higher or lower in status.

All of this has been borne out of a shared sense of empathy for other human beings. You will find that having empathy will smooth the waters, not only for yourself but also for others.

Of course, there are a small percentage of people who take advantage of this empathy. I do not mean the criminal element; I refer instead to the professional unemployed. There are others who rort the workers' compensation system, but these people are a minority, and we should not judge the majority based upon them. When economic conditions are strong, unemployment levels can drop to around 4 per cent. This demonstrates that 96 per cent of people want to work and perhaps another 2 per cent are in the process of changing jobs. Even the remaining 2 per cent are not necessarily rorting the system but may remain unemployable due to any number of reasons.

Let us not forget that greatness is frequently achieved by people who show an immense amount of "goodliness" and "Godliness", including David Livingstone, Albert Schweitzer and Mother Teresa of Calcutta. The man I admire the most in the modern era, Nelson Mandela, was the first to move forward and instigate reconciliation in spite of his appalling treatment by the forces of Apartheid.

CHAPTER 2

LEARN THE SET-UP

1. THE BASIC LAWS

The Law of Ignorance

In 1984, I moved from Victoria to South Australia. Driving along happily one day, I needed to make a U-turn. At the next set of lights, I pulled over to the centre of the road, indicated to turn right, allowed an oncoming police car to pass and then executed the U-turn. A police officer saw this, waved me down and booked me for doing a U-turn at a traffic light. I explained that I was from Victoria and did not know it was against the law in South Australia. Did my ignorance of the law put me above the law? No. Ignorance of the law is not an excuse you can hide behind to escape your responsibility. With the law, as with many other matters, you are required to find out for yourself. It is not anyone else's responsibility to tell you.

A friend and I were discussing an opportunity for him to set up a manufacturing business. Knowing a little of his position, I said, "But Tom, where are you going to find the money?" He said, "I don't need much." I then explained to him that in order to achieve the level of sales he expected, he needed money to buy raw materials, pay overheads and wages. He then had to finance his finished product stock and carry his customers' debt until he was paid. His jaw dropped and, amazed, he said to me, "Why didn't somebody tell me?"

Tom was thirty-five years old and had held senior positions in various companies. He was a big boy, yet he sincerely believed it was someone else's responsibility to tell him what he needed to know. In his own mind, he had absolved himself of any responsibility. Don't make this mistake. Accept the responsibility of getting to know the set-up.

You don't necessarily have to like the set-up, but you have to know it. There are two reasons for this. First of all, you will avoid being burned. Secondly, it will teach you to get on the 'plus side'.

The Law of Inertia

Newton's law states, "A body will resist being brought into motion, but once in motion will resist being brought to a stop." Imagine there is a huge, heavy flywheel sitting stationary. It takes an immense amount of power and effort to get that flywheel moving. Once it starts moving, it takes less effort to get it to go faster. Once it has worked up to a certain speed, it takes a huge amount of effort to stop it.

We are like that flywheel. Initially, we resist change and even oppose it, but once started in motion we often gain momentum and move at such a speed that nothing will stop us. Your attitude is your flywheel, and your personal development through knowledge is the force that will drive the flywheel into motion. You must learn to use your knowledge. There are two rules that you must remember and apply:

- Whatever you don't use, you lose
- Whatever you don't invest, you forfeit

The Law of Growing

Whatever you sow, you reap. If you don't sow, you can't reap. There are seven significant points in the Law of Growing:

- **Negative**—If you are negative, you will see negatives. I'm sure you have met many people in your life who have become totally absorbed in a negative attitude. This way of thinking is a habit that is not broken because these people cannot, will not or do not recognise that they are negative. When something goes wrong, the problem must be recognised. From then on, the object is to do something about it, to take a positive action developed from a positive mental attitude. Do yourself a very big favour: do not wish your life away waiting for it to be better. Do something about it now.

- **Positive**—As you think, so you will become. It is not easy to develop a positive attitude in life, yet the best way to do it is to stop thinking negatively. Behind every cloud, there is a rainbow. Look for the rainbow, not the rain.

- **Rewards**—You will always get out more than you put in. Likewise, the more you take out the more you will lose. There are many rewards: happiness, wealth, children, family, pleasure, fulfillment, achievement. The list is almost infinite.

- **Many ways**—If all roads lead to Rome, there must be many different ways to get to Rome. Life is a maze and we all must find our way through it. Sometimes we find ourselves at the end of a blind alley from which we must retreat in order to find a way to the exit. You will never walk through the maze of life without sometimes coming to a blind alley.

- **You can do it, too**—Next year you will arrive somewhere. Whether or not it is where you want to be is entirely up to you. If you do not follow a road map, you will end up somewhere you do not want to be, a long way from your destination.

- **Sometimes you may crash**—It is unusual for someone to go through life without having at least one crash, whether major or minor. If you drive with anticipation, you will minimise crashes and they will not prove fatal.

- **Decide whether to go**—If you don't go, you will stay where you are. If that pleases you, do not complain about your lack of movement.

2.   THE ROAD TO SUCCESS

You have a journey ahead of you that is going to take a lifetime. You won't get to your desired destination unless you have enough fuel. The first question is, "Do you want to make a living or would you like to design a life?" If you choose the latter then you have to set both short—and long-term goals. Your long-term goals, at this stage, may be your dreams. Only you can turn your dreams into next year's reality.

Fill the tank

Your motives will be the fuel that sustains you throughout your journey. When your motives are negative, they become excuses. When your motives are positive, they become the driving force.

You can achieve anything you want in life, provided you have the right motives. Conversely, if your goals remain unfulfilled, it is almost certainly because you did not have enough of a reason to fulfill them. It is always a person's motives that drive them to their ultimate achievement—and they can be limitless.

For example, Smith left the pub one night at 10.30pm, five sheets to the wind, when he found it was raining cats and dogs. Instead of taking his normal route home, he decided to take a shortcut through a graveyard. He was hurrying in the darkness through the rain when he accidentally fell into a newly dug grave. He tried to climb out but was only able to claw and slide on the wet, muddy sides of the grave. After about thirty minutes of intense exertion, he flopped, exhausted, into the corner and resolved to remain there until morning. After about ten minutes, he heard footsteps hurrying through the graveyard. It was Jones, who fell into the same grave. He picked himself up and began the seemingly impossible task of climbing out of the grave. After a while, Smith said to Jones, "You'll never get out of here!" But Jones did.

The difference between the two was that Jones had a reason to get out. You don't need more intelligence, but you do need a reason. You will not have all the answers and it's doubtful you ever will. That is unimportant.

Reasons come first. Answers come second.

Your reasons for achieving personal development fall into three main categories:

- Personal—These are your own motives for doing something. It could be for recognition or respect. It may be just for the thrill of winning. Often people who become wealthy do so as a by-product of winning. They don't necessarily set out to become wealthy, but the sheer joy of winning sustains them. People who get joy from winning are often accused of being greedy because they never seem to have enough. This is often a misjudgment.
- Family—People may do things not for themselves, but for their families. It may be for their children, in order to provide them with more than they had themselves.
- Benevolence—For some, their motive is the act of sharing. After Andrew Carnegie died, someone found a note in his desk saying, "I have spent one half of my life making a great deal of money and the other half giving it away."

The question is, "What do you need to turn you on?" Or, conversely, "What has turned you off?"

Get into the vehicle

Your long-term goals are your dreams. They may seem totally unreachable now, but if you are to go anywhere you must have them.

When I fit myself into the Seven zones of comfort (outlined in a later chapter of this book), I recognise that I am a Climber. I have my long-term dreams but I focus only on the next step. Once I have climbed there, I focus on the next step again. In time, I will fulfill all the dreams I originally may have had at Step Five. Once there, I develop a new set of dreams and again and climb those steps until they are fulfilled.

Your dreams can change; you can reassess yourself at any time. You can alter your course to go around obstacles but you can't put the vehicle in reverse. Let me tell you, you can't go backwards. Certainly, you may come off the rails at times, but that is a temporary setback. Mentally, you will drive yourself forward. In life, we often take two steps forward and one step back. Never believe that a backward step is permanent.

Personal development and success is not a matter of intelligence but inspiration. If intelligence were the only qualifier then academics would be rich. In fact, it is quite often the reverse. Most academics are middle-income earners; people without formal education more often become wealthy. To be inspired, you must be able to visualise what you want. This brings us back to our dreams. Revenge is often a reason to inspire us to aspire, and there is no better revenge than massive success.

Turn the key

Decision time. You can't sit in your car with the engine off and expect to get somewhere. You must first decide to turn the key. It's as simple as that. I cannot tell you what to do; I can only tell you how to do it. *You* must decide for yourself.

Make today 'Decision Day'. Write your decision down. Once you have it on paper, you have made the decision. You are committed. If you haven't written it out, do so as a mark of your commitment to self-development.

Undertake the journey

Let me tell you the secret of having anything in life you want: ASK!

- Ask and you shall receive. The biggest obstacle standing in the way of a person achieving what they want is to be "no"-shy. It is amazing the fear that this two-letter word conjures up. People who are "no"-shy will go to great lengths to avoid situations where someone may say, "No."
- For a salesperson, it is unacceptable to be "no"-shy. If you are afraid to ask, you can never, never succeed in a selling career. You may think that simply to ask is an over-simplification. You are right, it is.

The first step is for you to *accept* the concept that you can get anything you want if you ask. The second step is to learn to ask properly. Asking is the beginning of receiving, but receiving is not the problem. Don't work on receiving; receiving is automatic. Believe me, it is like an ocean; there is so much of it to share. If you have decided to take a trip to the ocean don't take a teaspoon, take a bucket.

There are two ways to ask for what you want:

Ask with intelligence—Describe what you want. Help the person you are asking to visualise what you want. If you are trying to sell them something, you must ask them to visualise it for themselves, then when they get what they want, you will get what you want.

Ask with faith—Believe with your body and soul that you can get what you want. If you cannot believe it yourself, how can you expect the other person to believe?

Let's be clear about this. There are no guarantees that you are going to get what you want by asking. In fact, you definitely will not get everything you want, but the odds weigh much more heavily in your favour than if you had not asked.

Obstacles on the way

For me, the greatest political joke is the idea of the 'level playing field'. There is no such animal. You are never going to get a smooth ride all the way; obstacles are going to occur to impede your progress. The obstacles that cannot be removed must be circumnavigated. These are usually external obstacles.

In reality, it is your attitude that will create the greatest hurdles. These you *can* change; you have the power. In fact, only you have it.

Be on guard for the 'diseases of attitude'. What do you do when you have a disease? You give yourself the properly prescribed medication or you surgically remove the problem.

The Diseases of Attitude

- **Indifference**—Indifference means lack of care: care for yourself, your family, your friends, your job, your attitude, your life. Don't let indifference rob you of a good life.
- **Complacency**—Nowhere is this more apparent than within relationships. In the modern world, the divorce rate is around 50 per cent. Of the remaining 50 per cent, I would say 30 per cent are not happy. One of the single biggest reasons for this is complacency. When two people meet, they will put on a "show" and do things they may not ordinarily do. However, the longer they are in a relationship the less effort they make until one day they wake up to find they are not living with the same person they married. This is complacency at its worst. Don't let complacency destroy your relationships.
- **Indecision**—This mental paralysis of indecision can only be cured by making a decision. Even a bad decision is better than no decision at all.
- **Worry**—When you don't make a plan, failure comes as a surprise because it is not preceded by long periods of worry and doubt. Do not worry about what might happen. Take out insurance by planning your life.
- **Over-cautiousness**—People often say, "It is risky." Life is risky: as the saying goes, you will never get out of it alive. The reality is that risk is ever-present and there is absolutely no way of avoiding it. What you can do is minimise risk by developing an active sense of anticipation.
- **Pessimism**—The pessimist sees difficulty in opportunity, whereas the optimist sees opportunity in difficulty. Pessimism is a direct result of having a negative attitude. Stop thinking about what is wrong with your life and start thinking about what is right.
- **Complaining**—If you complain long enough you will have your future cancelled.

For a moment, let's re-examine risk. There is no avoiding risk. Everything in life is risky. There is always risk of an accident, risk of losing and a risk of being ill. Let the record show that you won or lost, but never let it show that you didn't play because you were afraid of the risks.

Do you want to know the secret of being positive? It is simple: stop being negative. Isn't being negative a self-fulfilling prophecy? Don't be frightened of your emotions, because they can turn your life around. Emotions are often a powerful trigger to progress.

Arrive at your destination

Research carried out to identify high achievers has found that they have eight traits in common:

- They go beyond previous levels of achievement by competing against themselves
- They know what they want and have clear and specific strategies for getting it
- They have a high tolerance for uncertainty and deal well with confusing situations from which others would flee
- They draw few distinctions between work and play—work is often their hobby
- They are rarely sick and seldom take a day off
- They solve problems rather than look for blame
- They confidently take risks after weighing up the worst possible consequences of an action
- They avoid comfort zones where others get stuck

Here is an important quote for you: "Fear is the energy when I do my best work."—Barbra Streisand

Don't just read it; think about it. Don't just think about it; absorb it.

When you feel butterflies in your stomach, when you feel your 'nakedness' as you move out of your comfort zone, when you feel your fear about to overwhelm you, recognise those feelings as signals that you might be about to do something better than you have ever done in your life.

If you don't get that fear at least once a month you are probably stationary. Fear is the anticipation of stepping into strange territory, and discovery is rewarded by the exhilaration of success.

CHAPTER 3

THE JOURNEY

At the age of twenty-six, I moved up to the next step on my 'stairway' and became a General Manager of Operations. While my ambitions were being fulfilled—indeed, with great difficulty, as I was hanging on like grim death—I found I had a problem. I had too much month left at the end of my money.

Some people can make a difference to you, providing you have your mind tuned in. I was working with a delightful gentleman named Mr. Julius Rosenberg. He was like a father to me and I appreciated him greatly. Mr. Rosenberg told me something that made a huge difference in my life: "From today, stop going to work on your job and start going to work on yourself. Work harder on yourself than you do on your job and I guarantee you will fulfill your own expectations, as well as everyone else's."

I did just that. From that day on, I gave up work and went to work on myself. I haven't looked back.

If you go to work on yourself with a development plan, success will automatically happen. Yet there is something even more important: "It is not what you *get* that makes you happy. It is what you *become*."

In the 1960s, enthusiasm was put forward as the key to personal development. Baloney! No matter how much I danced and pranced and flapped my arms, I could never fly at all. Enthusiasm may be a necessary and admirable quality, but it is not going to get you there. You have to go to work on yourself. Do yourself a favour. In the diary note I asked you to make earlier marking your career's birthday, write, "The day I went to work on myself. "Commemorate that date every year. It will be a constant reminder of your need to develop yourself and it will be a day to reward yourself for what you have done in the past year.

Let's take a journey down the road of personal development. Let's examine where you want to go and how you can get there with certainty.

<u>Ideas</u>

In the mid-1970s, Michael Draper, a businessman in Auckland, engaged me for a week to consult on his business restructure. One of the components of the restructure was to employ a new production manager. We interviewed a candidate called Brian, who asked Michael, "What is your attitude to people in the business who may have been there a long time, but are no longer contributing anything?" As quick a flash, Michael responded, "We do not keep and feed holy cows."

Throughout our lives, we are all exposed to many great ideas. We normally respond by saying, "That's a great idea. I must remember that." Mostly you don't. Why? Because you didn't write it down. That has to change. From today, take a notebook and mark on the front of it 'My Proverbial Collection'. Put it in your briefcase and every time someone gives you an idea, instead of trying to remember it, write it down. You are now creating your own log of ideas. Whenever you think of something significant, add it to your log.

I started my log years ago. You can read it at the end of this book. You may feel free to use some of the ideas there, but your own log will ultimately be very different from mine. Throughout my own personal development journey, my log of ideas has never failed me.

We are talking now of change. We are discussing a process which will go on throughout your life: constant change. For things to change for you, you have to change.

Productivity

Productivity will be discussed in detail the chapter "Working Smarter Not Harder". There is something, however, I wish to address now. Primarily, you get paid for value. You are not paid for time and effort. Value makes all the difference in results.

Another thing needs to be understood: don't spend major amounts of time on minor concerns. Don't let minor things worry you or distract you from major tasks.

Handling Change

Change will not come naturally; it is something that has to be learned. The first and most vital step is to learn what can be changed and what cannot. Don't, under any circumstances, waste your time working on things that are not within your power to change. Work on the things you *can* change.

I am a disciple of change and totally dedicated to it, but even I recognise that there are many things that cannot be changed. In the 6,000 years of recorded history many things have remained the same. Every day the sun has come up in the morning and gone down in the evening. Every month the moon has gone through its cycle. Every year the world has completely circled the sun. These and many other things will never be changed, at least not by you or me.

The rules of the road

Life is like the ever-changing conditions of the road. You can't change the road but you can change yourself. There are four rules associated with change. Learn them.

RULE 1—Sometimes the Road Gets Rough

There will always be periods in all our lives when the road gets rough. When it happens, do not wish it was easier, train yourself to be better. Do not ask for fewer problems, because they will not go away until you have faced and solved them. As you do so, you will experience a surprising side effect: the development of new skills.

Your life will be filled with problems and that won't change. It's your attitude towards those problems that can change. Remember, problems are difficulties that impede the progress of others. All you have to do is make sure that you are not one of the others.

RULE 2—Push ahead when the road becomes smooth

Rough roads don't go on forever. While you are on them it seems like they will never end, but there will always come a smooth stretch. Don't let this opportunity pass you by. Most people do, their attitude being, "That was a rough time but now I can relax." However, this is not the time to simply enjoy the scenery but to press your foot down on the accelerator and surge ahead, taking full advantage of the better conditions.

You may have had to mark time when the road was rough, now is the time to capitalise on your fortune. Even if you fail to grasp it at that moment, remember there will be more than one smooth stretch in your life. I'm not encouraging you to let opportunities slip through your fingers but if they do, remember that there will be others. It's like a retail bargain that panics people into buying. Bargains will occur again next week, next month and next year.

RULE 3—Learn to anticipate dangers on the way

All that is good will be attacked because others want it for themselves. Everything of value must be defended. It is predictable that others will want to take things from you. Be proactive and keep important things in your peripheral vision.

RULE 4—On arrival, enjoy the experience without complaint

You have to take full responsibility for the result of your actions, whether good or bad. If you do well, accept it without apology to others. If you haven't done so well, don't complain.

Opportunity is always mixed with difficulty—that will not change. Anything worth having is difficult. Indeed, if it weren't difficult, it wouldn't provide an opportunity. Things do not happen by chance, they happen because you have planned the change. It is what you do that will make the difference. If you do nothing, nothing will happen.

One of the ideas in my log is, "Losers fight; winners fly over the top." Don't fight the things you cannot change. Accept them and go around them. Instead, fight the things you *can* change. Be in the front line as a leader and implement change, otherwise you are just a follower. What are you going to do today that will make a difference?

Drivers

There are two drivers toward success: discipline and motivation. But what you must recognise is that there can be only one kind of each: *SELF*-DISCIPLINE AND *SELF*-MOTIVATION.

Don't look for someone else to motivate you. How often have you heard people say, "I'm not motivated"? They are complaining that someone else is not providing motivation and discipline for them. Motivation is up to you.

Discipline yourself to be effective with your time and guard it well. Resent every second you or someone else wastes. Time itself means nothing but time mixed with skill and method is everything.

Personally, I am so time-conscious that people call me Microwave Man (although I would have preferred Superman!). I am Microwave Man because I compress everything I do into the smallest span of time. If we installed an open fire, it would have to be a microwave fireplace so instead of relaxing in front of it all evening I could do it in ten minutes.

Watch for the danger signals. If you begin to think you need someone to discipline or motivate you, you are taking a significant step backwards.

If you wish to improve your lot in life commence with the understanding that it is entirely up to you. No one else can make that decision for you and no one else can provide the discipline and motivation needed to achieve what you want to achieve.

Knowledge

It is almost certain that the process of self-development will make you a leader. Even if you don't design your program to make you one, it will surely happen. To be a good leader, you have to be a good *reader*.

Educate yourself, but remember that a standard education gets standard results. It's essential that you spend at least thirty minutes each day reading. Make this a habit, like your morning shower, and never miss out on your thirty minutes.

I read for thirty minutes before going to sleep each night. In this way, not only do I fulfill my reading objective, but the subject is subconsciously processed during my sleep and I invariably wake up with a good idea.

All successful people are readers. If you don't have a book collection, start your own library today. Don't ask how much it costs—books are the best form of knowledge and education you can possibly obtain.

Don't develop 'TV Syndrome'. Many people who fail can be identified by the fact that they know every TV program on during the week. Even if the programs are all boring, they won't switch off the television and do something interesting but instead switch channels until they find the best of the bad lot. They treat their minds like dustbins. The important question is: Are you?

Above all else, *listen, observe and ask questions*. Success leaves clues. If people are successful, look for the clues to their success and follow them. Listen to what people say. Poorer people often resent the rich, but rather than wasting time on bitterness they should instead be asking wealthy people questions and actively listening to the secrets of their success.

We learn by observation. There are two ways you can observe: through sight and through *in*sight.

Planning

I repeat that you will only ever succeed on purpose, never by chance. Having a plan means implementing change.

As a starting point, sit down and decide on the income you would like to achieve. It is OK for this to be a dream figure. Remember, if you throw a ball at a target you must aim higher to account for the ball's gravitational trajectory. Therefore, always start with a higher amount. Then decide upon the action you need to take to achieve that goal, remembering that the higher you aim the greater your trajectory and the more likely you are to hit your target.

Take action on the information you already have. Build on that information base so you can develop another plan in a year's time, based on the knowledge you have gained. Take action on your plan, but if you feel the change is not quick enough, be prepared to take massive action. Massive action gets massive results. Smaller actions get fewer results.

Remember only to change the things you *can* and not the things you can't. Don't be stubborn. If something isn't working, jettison it.

Decision-making

Julius Rosenberg's son, Essex, was a partner and mentor of mine. I owe Essex a huge debt of gratitude for helping me become a decision maker. During the early 1970s, we spent a hard year working together to build a brand new factory that employed seventy people. Two weeks after we had commenced distribution of our product he walked into my office and said, "Tomorrow, I am going overseas for six weeks. My in-tray is empty now and it will be empty when I come back. *If you have a problem, make a decision, because even a wrong decision is better than no decision at all.*"

Do you think that didn't go into my log? From that moment on, I never had a problem making a decision. Essex's advice made me a very efficient decision maker. When I did something wrong I was able to accept it immediately and make another decision to put it right. It is the fear of making a bad decision that stops people from making decisions at all.

Don't think you will get it right all the time. If you get it right 51 per cent of the time, you are winning. You are going to make some—maybe many—wrong decisions. Accept that and move on. The only person who never made a wrong decision is the person who never made a decision at all.

Here are some guidelines which have helped me enormously. Whilst there are an infinite variety of steps in the decision-making process, I have set myself three simple rules:

1. When you are pretty sure, be decisive with a yes or a no
2. When you are unsure, give yourself time to consider the decision and set a deadline
3. When you are doubtful, the answer is no

Understand, people who are indecisive will always say no because, "No is safe."

CHAPTER 4

THE COMFORT SYNDROME

It is critical that you always try to understand and approach your issues from new angles. Even if you have been in business for twenty years, it is never too late to start doing this.

The first thing you should do is open your diary at today's date and write in big capitals 'DAY ONE'. This represents your career's birthday. It means that as of today your career has been reborn. It should be celebrated each year to serve as a reminder and reinforce everything you are going to change and apply.

The first step on the road of personal development is for you to identify where you are now. Ask yourself, "Is this where I want to stay?" If your answer is "No," then you need to understand some of the mind shifts that will help you to develop a different mind-set.

This is what personal development is all about. If you have arrived where you are today by pure chance, how much more successful will you be if you start doing things on purpose? The fact that you are investing your time in reading this book is a strong indication that you want to move forward. I would suggest that you are almost certainly of a mind set to want to develop yourself. This can only be achieved by finding the energy to undergo a mind shift.

First of all, we need to examine the 'comfort syndrome' into which we all fit, one way or another. This will help explain what we are, where we are and why we are here. I will take you through a four-stage process, which I liken to the enjoyment of a good bottle of wine.

First, take out the cork

We all have our personal comfort zones. Your comfort zone may be my *discomfort* zone. If your comfort zone is on a level above mine, then I will feel uncomfortable moving myself out of my zone to attain your level. The opposite can also apply. If you are on a level below me, I will feel equally uncomfortable if I attempt to join you there. None of us like to go backwards.

When we take ourselves out of our comfort zones we place ourselves either in a situation where we want to be, but haven't achieved yet, or in a situation we don't want to be in at all. So it is necessary to make one assumption before we proceed: wherever you are in the hierarchy, you want to go higher.

By staying in our comfort zone we place one of the greatest of all limitations on ourselves. There are exceptions to this: people whose comfort zone is, in fact, their *discomfort* zone. These are the people who strive for excellence. They are uncomfortable sitting still and cannot accept the way things are now. They want to be better than they are now. They are described as having drive and ambition.

Let us establish that a comfort zone can have three effects on you: negative, neutral or positive.

Personal development can take you in whatever direction you wish to go. For some, it may mean earning more money. For others, it may mean being more "goodly" by being more "Godly". Many academics strive for knowledge and many mothers have an instinctive need to be a better parent. Whatever your own personal destination, there is always a reward at the end.

One of the major drivers of success is income. Let me tell you something that I have observed and learned: income does not far exceed personal development.

No matter where people work, they each have an earnings plateau I call their 'comfort level'. Each individual's comfort level varies. For Fred Smith it may be $40,000 per year, for Ian Jones it may be $80,000 per year and for me it may be unlimited. People set their comfort level at whatever they can visualise as their contentment level.

This is not to be confused with their *satisfaction* level. Fred Smith's satisfaction level may be to buy his own four bedroom home, two cars, two television sets, a microwave and a dog. Fred and his wife will strive to achieve those items. They will work hard, work overtime and sacrifice lifestyle until they get what they want, but once they have them, they are not prepared to sacrifice for very much more.

Fred Smith may have his home, two cars, two television sets, microwave and dog but his boss wants him to work all day Saturday. For this, he is paid overtime at penalty rates. Let's assume he pays the top tax rate. Fred figures that working all day Saturday, missing out on his relaxation, his football and a drink with his mates is not worth the extra money he can earn after paying tax. He is in his comfort zone, and the benefits required to motivate him out of his zone have to be far greater. The problem also is that he doesn't *visualise beyond his comfort zone*, so he believes the extra effort is not worthwhile.

Previously, I used the terms *comfort level* and *satisfaction level* separately. Fred is not satisfied, but he is content. He would like a better house, a Mercedes Benz and overseas trips but he either believes that the amount of effort required to achieve them puts them beyond his reach or he cannot visualise them for himself. In fact, in the egalitarian world of today there is frequently an expectation that someone else, often the Government, will provide it for us.

This is demonstrated particularly clearly in the welfare system. Governments will set the unemployment benefit at a level that will sustain people without making them rich. If too little is paid, someone, perhaps the children of families on welfare, will suffer. On the other hand, if too much is paid then people may fail to see the object of working and decide to live off the state, even though that invariably means going without luxuries. It is very fortunate that only a small percentage of the population thinks this way (my best guess is around 2 per cent). I find very encouraging because it means 98 per cent of people are not prepared to accept that level of existence and are prepared to work for more.

Therefore, we must conclude that most people, particularly at the beginning of their working lives, will strive to move out of their comfort zone to achieve their goals and will only settle into their comfort zone once their immediate needs are satisfied. At that time they achieve contentment but not necessarily satisfaction; they would still like a better car, better holidays, a better home, a better education for their children. There are a multitude of things that could improve their lives but they are no longer prepared to make the sacrifices to achieve them.

Understanding the comfort zone is one of the most significant factors in achieving success. People who have no ceiling on their comfort zone, who can visualise the benefits of unlimited success, are the ones who acknowledge their potential and become the leaders in our society.

Comfort has two dimensions: comfort *level* and comfort *zone.*

We can best visualise these two dimensions not as a square, but as a letter 'Z'. The top and the bottom of the Z represent different comfort levels, while the angled line connecting them represents the various comfort zones between the two levels.

I have identified seven distinct zones. The category into which a person fits is recognisable by that person's attitude.

Comfort zones represent the many shades of grey between the levels. In other words, you may be on the ground floor but you could be on the bottom step of the stairway that takes you to the next level.

The attitude you develop determines where you are in that hierarchy. The velocity of your personal development determines the change in your attitude, which in turn manifests itself in how quickly you move up or down that hierarchy. You can develop slowly, step by step, moving cautiously from one comfort zone to another and, in time, reach a different level or you can move dynamically and take a quick shift from one level to another. Some people who are extraordinarily motivated and gifted will take quantum leaps.

Understand that you are in control of the motor providing the energy that builds the momentum. You can choose to take the stairs, or to go by the lift. The lift requires a greater mind shift but, in fact, less energy is ultimately used.

You are not born into any level. Comfort zones and levels are a by-product of your attitude, which can be a by-product of your environmental influences. Certainly, it is quite common for the higher levels to be rewarded with income and wealth, but that does not necessarily follow. Neither does it follow that all movement is upward. If you switch your motor off, you will begin to sink. This is important because it recognises that at least you must have your motor turning over just to maintain a static position in life.

If you are sitting in your car in the driveway, you have four choices once you have switched the motor on. You can put the car into reverse and go backwards until you hit the wall. You can sit there with the engine idling, which at least maintains most of the working parts and uses little fuel. You can move the shift into forward drive and move ahead at whatever speed you desire, depending upon the pressure you exert on the accelerator or you can choose the fourth option. You can choose to switch the engine off and sit there, in which case both you and the car will slowly deteriorate.

Getting ahead in life doesn't mean you have had a comfort zone shift. Life is not a static thing. Most people progress through life and change without necessarily moving out of their comfort zone. It is a natural progression, but that progression is limited and subtle. A comfort zone shift is a dynamic move from one zone or level to another, precipitated by your attitude. Before we can move forward we must examine our needs, wants and desires.

Needs

Needs are the essentials of existence. Ever heard someone tell you that their basic needs have been catered for? Our needs are food, shelter and clothing, and to me that means survival. In other words, if only your basic needs are catered for you are not 'living' but merely surviving. Survival is the most basic state of human existence. For many people, that is all they want to do. This is generally because to do more than simply survive means getting out of their comfort zone.

While many people in this category will be content, the majority will not. It is a hallmark of human nature that people will rarely take responsibility for their own actions.

For example, you may be driving on a road, following another car which for whatever reason abruptly stops. Consequently, you drive into the back of this car. Many people would blame the first driver for stopping, irrespective of the reason for the stop. For example, a child may run across the road in front of the first driver, in which case he will reactively slam on his breaks. Should the first driver take the responsibility for the person running into the back of him? No. It is the obligation of the second driver to make sure there is an adequate stopping distance between themselves and the person in front, because at any time an emergency stop may occur. Additionally, it is the obligation of the second driver to ensure they are driving at a safe speed. Finally, it is the obligation of the second driver to be fully attentive to the driving conditions. In spite of this, the second driver will often blame the first.

Why is this so? The first and natural reaction for most people is to blame. This means they are not prepared to accept responsibility for their own actions. What is more, by rejecting blame they are absolving themselves from responsibility for their own lives. The law will always blame the second driver for causing the accident. However, most people would not accept that. When something happens that is not so black and white they take even less responsibility. If you wish to grow, you first have to take responsibility for your own actions which will later grow into an ability to take responsibility for others' actions as well. That is what leaders do.

In the modern world, particularly in developed countries, the old capitalist-versus-worker attitude is all but dead. Today, even the most right-wing societies still have socialist influences, with the state providing a safety net that ensures all but the extremely unfortunate are provided for.

As a result, the rich are not quite as rich because they are heavily taxed and the poor are not quite as poor because a safety net has been created.

Communism was a failed theory. It did not result in the equal distribution of wealth but in the unequal distribution of poverty because communism removed the two vital elements from society: incentive and initiative. It is these two elements that are powered by people moving out of their comfort zone.

Consider this. If the ability to grow is removed from society, people will not try because there is no point in them doing so. They will do what they have to in order to survive. Likewise, if initiative is removed from society then people will not have any incentive to improve their lives.

During Mao's "Great Leap Forward", thirty million people were estimated to have died from starvation. What is more, trees and other combustible materials were used to feed backyard furnaces until there was ecological devastation. The great communist Deng Xiaoping recognised peoples' need for incentive and initiative. They needed the ability to improve both themselves and society. Recognising that the only successful economic model was a free market economy Deng Xiaoping gradually eased his foot off the brake by allowing peasants to farm unused land to grow products they could sell at a profit. As a result, China is now the second biggest economy in the world, almost five times the size of that of the US. This means that China need only achieve a per capita income one fifth of the USA's to become the most powerful country in the world, economically speaking. That is what results from giving people incentive and initiative.

<u>Wants</u>

Everyone strives to have their needs met because we cannot survive without them. Beyond our needs are our wants. Most people want more than the basic needs but not all people are prepared to move out of their comfort zone to achieve their wants. As a result they remain static in life, unfulfilled, and often resentful of the people who have achieved their wants. Nevertheless, wanting something more is the trigger that will result in a shift of your comfort zone. The shift depends on the degree of your wants. A big want is a big ask, which requires a big comfort zone shift. People who do this are often described as having 'drive'.

While our needs can be easily satisfied, our wants require more effort. If you are to achieve your wants you are going to have to move out of your comfort zone. The degree of this shift will depend on the size of your want. The bigger the want, the bigger the shift required. As soon as you say to yourself, "I want that," you are signaling a change. The amount you move depends on the nature of your want.

For example, to say, "I want more bread," means that you want more of the same. However, to say, "I want something better than bread," probably indicates a comfort zone shift. Just as catering for our needs make us content, catering to our wants will satisfy us at least until such time as we want more.

Desires

Our desires are the real motivators. Our needs and wants will make us feel content, but not satisfied. Our desires create the appetite that is satisfied only by fulfilling our dreams. When our dreams are fulfilled, they are often replaced by other dreams that need fulfilling, like a carrot dangling on a stick.

It is not what we need or want that will move us out of our comfort zone, but what we desire. No one wants to be poor or remain poor. Most of us would prefer to be wealthy but not all of us are prepared to make the sacrifices needed to create wealth. We have to realise it is not our lack of desire but our disinclination to make sacrifices that holds us back. The major sacrifice we make is moving out of our comfort zone. Of course, many people say it is not important but often the same people will go out and buy a lottery ticket. In other words, they are saying, "Yes, I want to be wealthy but I'm not prepared to make the sacrifices. If I am lucky enough, the lottery ticket I buy will make me wealthy without having to shift out of my comfort zone."

I'm only using wealth as an example. Rarely will wealth itself be the motivator as it is very often a by-product of success, achieved by moving out of your comfort zone.

Now, pour the wine

The fulcrum of our personal development is attitude.

Professor Julius Sumner-Miller said that the three greatest minds the world has ever known were Archimedes, Newton and Einstein. He personally thought Archimedes was the greatest. My point is not to debate that issue, but to examine what Archimedes identified.

Archimedes discovered the "mathematics of moments". He used leverage to develop all sorts of devices, including war machines. What he achieved is embodied in his profound statement, "Give me a place to stand and I will move the world."

Leverage has two components: the lever and the fulcrum. The heavier the object you want to move, the closer you must place the fulcrum to the object and the greater the leverage you can exert to move it. Attitude is the fulcrum of your personal development. The worse your attitude, the further the fulcrum will be from what you want to move and the greater the effort required to obtain a small degree of personal development. The better the attitude, the smaller the effect required to achieve a massive change. Therefore, examine your attitude to give you clues as to why you are not achieving what you want to achieve. Often it is because you do not have enough reason, fortitude or self-discipline to make that change.

It can be a long process. Learning to play the piano is not achieved in one lesson but takes years of application and practice. However, it is the desire to learn to play that provides the fortitude to carry you through all those years of practice. Given the right reasons you can achieve anything—even the seemingly impossible.

<u>Influences</u>

We all have to play the cards we are dealt by the big card dealer in the sky. We cannot change our hand, but we can learn to play it better.

We cannot eliminate what we are or what we have, but if we have enough desire we can learn to become what want to be. Many people are born with horrific disabilities. Some blame the world for their ills, which makes them worse off for having that attitude. Many accept the hand they are dealt and get on with making their lives as normal as possible. Others heroically overcome their disabilities and achieve greatness for themselves, irrespective of whether or not their achievements are recognised.

One of the finest examples of this is Professor Stephen Hawking. He took over from where Einstein left off as a cosmologist, and was the co-discoverer of Black Holes and the shape of the universe. In his early twenties, he suffered a life-threatening disease and was given two years to live. His body has since deteriorated to a point where many normal functions, including speech, are not possible.

None of this has limited his achievements in the slightest. He writes books and delivers lectures despite the fact that he cannot speak. He uses a computer coupled to a voice simulator to communicate with the world and has produced some of humanity's most advanced thinking. His attitude has allowed him to overcome horrific difficulties, leading him to supreme personal development.

What I am saying is that you cannot change the fact that you may be only five-foot-three. But that doesn't have to stop you walking tall.

If you feel, "I cannot help being the person I am," you are wrong. What has really happened is that you haven't found sufficient reason to change yourself. People always have so many reasons: "The reason I can't do this is . . ." or "The reason I didn't is . . ." Reasons and excuses have the same meaning. Instead of finding excuses as to why you can't do something, start looking for reasons you can. The difference between the two is simply attitude. And attitude is not genetic, but a product of your environmental conditioning.

We are all a product of two factors: our genetics and our environment. These two combine to shape our attitude and it is our attitude which moulds what we become.

Environmental influences

From as far back as I can remember, whenever I said to my grandmother, "I can't . . ." she would always say, "There is no such word as 'can't'." This was drilled into me day after day, month after month, year after year and today I consider there is nothing I can't do. My grandmother removed 'can't' from my agenda. I don't know how much this influenced what I am today, or how it helped me overcome some of the difficulties I have faced, but it is certainly a fine example of how your environment can influence you.

Your genes provide you with your basic operating system. But it is life that moulds you. One of the most common facets of human nature is displayed by parents who believe their child is still too young to be taught certain things. I believe the programming which takes place from birth up to the age of seven has the most profound influence. What you learn until that age will stay with you for the rest of your life. This doesn't mean you are locked in, but the job of reprogramming becomes more difficult the older you are. This does not mean you have finished learning, either. What it means is the foundations are being laid onto which you must build. It is all up to you and it is clearly your responsibility, so accept that responsibility and continue.

If you come from a negative background, it is more likely that your attitude will also be negative. If you were fortunate enough to be brought up in a positive environment, then you are more likely to be a positive person yourself. Your formative environment has a profound influence on what and who you are today.

If you want to change what you are, you can through personal development. The greatest thing about personal development is that anyone can do it. You don't have to be born into a personal development family. You too can join the club; all you have to do is ask *yourself* for membership. Personal development is one of the most satisfying things you can ever undertake.

Not only will it give you a sense of wellbeing, control and excellence, but it is likely your success will also grow.

Personal Development

You will only change things from what they are to what you want them to be through personal development. Your attitude controls your personal development, but who controls your attitude?

You do.

Again, let me be clear. Don't think I am trying to pull your strings. I don't need or want that responsibility. What I am saying is that if you want to change things from how they are to what you want them to be, you have to pull your *own* strings.

Now, drink the wine

The fact is that many people who sit in their comfort zones are exactly where they want to be. They are happy there and the last thing they want is for someone else to tell them they should move out. Everything is a matter of choice. You choose to be where you are. You may not have had an influence on where you began. You may not be responsible for the conditioning exerted by your environment. You may not be totally responsible for where you are today. But after reading this book, you will certainly be responsible for taking control of the rest of your life. You cannot abdicate the responsibility for your own personal development to others.

People fit logically into seven comfort zones. I haven't derived this from scientific analysis or psychological surveys, but from my own observations of human behaviour and drive. The percentage of people in each category has not been researched, nor is it important. The object of the exercise is to identify who they are, not how many there are.

My comments on each category are not intended to be critical or judgmental. I am simply attempting to make some elementary observations on the circumstances that are likely to identify the type. Please understand I am not in any way dictating where you or anyone else should be, nor am I commenting on your state of mind from the point of view of your level of happiness.

YOUR ATTITUDE DETERMINES YOUR ALTITUDE AND YOUR ALTITUDE DETERMINES YOUR SUCCESS.

The seven zones of comfort

LEVEL	ZONE	FORESIGHT	LIMITATION
Basement Two	Survivors	Next meal	Require basic needs because "it's all too hard"
Basement One	Needers	Next day	"I just need . . ."
Ground Floor	Commuters	Next week	Limited by desire
Level One	Drivers	Next month	Limited by vision—usually tunnel
Level Two	Climbers	Next year	Always look at the next step
Level Three	Visionaries	Next decade	See and focus on the top
Level Four	Flyers	Next lifetime	Unlimited and free to soar

Survivors

Survivors are at bottom of the food chain. These are the people whose basic needs of food, shelter and clothing are just met.

While some people in this category are there due to unfortunate circumstances beyond their control, many are there through choice. They were often born there and don't see beyond it. They don't move out of this zone, not because they are comfortable, but because they are not uncomfortable enough. To move out of their comfort zone is all too hard.

Survivors live from meal to meal. Others however have a burning need to change this. Because it is harder to work your way out of this zone your effort is greater and as a result your success can be spectacular. Let me remind you that Nelson Mandela was born in a black township in South Africa under Apartheid. He emerged from the horrors of twenty-seven years in prison to lead his nation to reconciliation. Nothing stopped Nelson Mandela from achieving his goals.

Needers

These are the ones whose comfort zone limitation is set because they have convinced themselves that "All I need is . . ." They require more than the survivors and are prepared to work to get more, but only enough to provide their needs. They may want to move out of their comfort zone, but have convinced themselves they can't for a variety of reasons.

With some it is because they may believe they are not worthy, with others it is because the effort is not worth it. Most common are the ones who incorrectly accept that this is their lot in life, and needlessly live from day to day. For example, they will shop almost daily because they lack the initiative to plan their meals ahead.

Commuters

Commuters are people who have caught the bus and are content to pay the fare to be driven around. Essentially, this is because they are limited by desire and are therefore generally content. They are an extremely important category, both socially and economically.

These people are the pillars of society, the salt of the earth. They are realistic, well balanced, and prepared to work hard and be happy. They are not just content, but satisfied with what they are and what they have.

Commuters will do a little forward planning. They are generally more concerned with what they are doing this week and will therefore shop on a weekly basis.

Drivers

These are people who have the ability and potential to go places, but are limited by their vision of themselves. They move forward, concentrating on the road immediately ahead, looking neither right nor left. If these people were inspired to see themselves in a different light, they would very easily move out of their comfort zone.

Drivers suffer from tunnel vision. Like racehorses, they wear blinkers, but the difference is that they put the blinkers on themselves. They will do their job with a great deal of focus and dedication. As a result, they are good to work with and are likely to make good supervisors. They are dependable and can be relied on to take and carry out instructions and directions without complaint.

Drivers plan their lives from month to month.

Climbers

Climbers move out of their comfort zone throughout their lives. They don't see themselves at, or look for, the 'top' but concentrate on the next step above them. Having climbed one step, they automatically look at the next.

If they stop climbing, they may have reached their discomfort zone, or they have chosen to say, "That's enough, I'm satisfied," and live out the remainder of their days happily.

Climbers can quite easily reach the top because they want to get out of their comfort zone and feel challenged. They are people who know exactly where they are, but may not yet have decided whether they want to stop.

Climbers will have this year's life planned ahead, with next year in their peripheral vision.

Visionaries

Visionaries have a clear vision of themselves at the top and possess the drive to get there. In this case, their comfort zone drives them to achieve their ambition because they are uncomfortable until such time as they get there.

Being a Visionary does not necessarily mean they are qualified to be at the top. There is no guarantee that they will get there but they will constantly drive themselves throughout their lives to achieve their place in the sun, irrespective of the number of failures and restarts it takes.

Confidence and self-assurance are some of the recognisable qualities of Visionaries, because they have their eye firmly fixed on the future. They recognise most of their inner qualities and will drive themselves to be the person required to fit their long-term vision. Ruthless people are more likely to be Visionaries than any other category. They have a clear focus and some don't mind what they have to do to get there, as long as they get there. The end justifies the means.

Strong-willed people are often Visionaries and their strength is usually misread as ruthlessness. There is a fine dividing line between the two. Margaret Thatcher, Golda Meir and Indira Gandhi were stamped with this misjudgment because they were women. To achieve what they achieved they had to be twice as strong as men.

Visionaries are usually self-controlled people, simply because their long-term plan is in place. They look ten years ahead.

Flyers

A select few people are totally unfettered by anything, even vision. They soar above in a rarefied atmosphere and often achieve either fame or infamy. They are uninhibited by their start in life and little obstructs their path. Some achieve greatness and history records them with respect, while others, like Hitler, Stalin, Saddam Hussein and Gaddafi, are noted with loathing.

Extremists are almost always flyers because of the qualities they possess in terms of mental toughness. Seldom is there any middle ground. They are either extremely good or extremely evil. Flyers can be extreme in their goodness. Mahatma Gandhi, David Livingstone, Albert Schweitzer and Mother Theresa were positive flyers because they had far more regard for others than for themselves. The negative flyers are the other extreme. They are totally and utterly evil, with little or no regard for anything other than their own demands. Flyers do not have a forward vision as we recognise it, but live in another world.

Now, appreciate the experience

This narrative should be useful to you in three ways. Firstly, you should sit back, audit yourself and assess where you fit in this hierarchy. Secondly, you should decide where you want to be, and thirdly, you need to make a plan to get there.

CHAPTER 5

Working Smarter, Not Harder

Have you ever wondered why some people work very hard and get nowhere while others just seem to coast through and do it easily? Why do other people make a lot of money when you are working just as hard, if not harder, and not getting anywhere near the same reward? For years you've heard people say, "Work smarter, not harder." I am going to be saying the same old thing, but I am going to tell you *how*.

There is so much talk today about productivity. Unions want wage increases for their workers, not just to keep up with the increase in the cost of living, but to create more disposable income and therefore improve their standard of living. Employers are not prepared to give more until they see some offsetting increase in productivity. The workers then think they are expected to wo3e3988urk harder for less pay. And so we have another round of industrial brinkmanship that is, in the end, the ultimate lose-lose situation.

Then the worst thing of all happens. The workers say, "They are putting in machines to do our jobs. We are going to lose them." If it isn't that, then it's, "They want to change work practices." And so another round of stop-work meetings and strikes begins. This represents change and we all resist change, some with more obstinacy than others.

The single biggest factor that stands between you and the fulfillment of your dreams and desires is your resistance to change.

When the first weaving and spinning machines were installed in Lancashire the hand spinners and weavers broke into factories and smashed the machines because they were afraid mechanisation would affect their job security. Those people were both resisting change and fearing the threat of new methods to their livelihood.

Since then, the world has undergone a far greater degree of mechanisation. Populations have increased greatly, yet today we are infinitely better off than we were two centuries ago. New machines and systems did not mean the loss of jobs but their creation. As mass production techniques were applied, quality improved and the cost of goods and services was reduced. Unemployment was kept in check despite the rapid growth of population, because the working week became shorter, holidays longer and weekends sacred.

This process transformed our standard of living into the one we enjoy today. Despite criticisms leveled at employers, Governments, unions and fellow-workers, we have never been better off. You are in danger of threatening your standard of living only when you resist change and stop progressing.

Let's go back to Lancashire during the Industrial Revolution. Rather than putting people out of work, the industrialisation of the textile industry produced 100s of thousands of jobs. Unfortunately, the mill owners did not pass on the benefits to their workers, which caused poor living standards and the creation of slums. The world was yet to learn of the free market economy and the benefits of a higher standard of living. A trickle of change from the rural to the urban environment soon turned into a tidal wave. England mass-produced textiles of a quality, quantity and price far better than any other country. Exports and fortunes grew, and jobs were created. At one time, there was a saying in Britain that, "England's bread hangs on Lancashire's thread."

Then the English committed the ultimate industrial sin: they rested on their laurels. For 100 years, the industry changed little, even though newer, faster and better machines were invented every decade. I know, because I was there for some of that time.

In 1959, I got my first job in a cotton mill at the age of fifteen. The equipment used had not changed for 200 years. They had the same old-fashioned weaving machines and no automatics. The spinning machines were still the same design as 200 years before, even though faster and better techniques had been developed in the meantime. That year, the British Government launched the Textile Industry Reorganisation Plan. They paid manufacturers to smash their machinery and go out of business so the small remaining market could be shared between the more efficient and productive companies. This spelled disaster for Lancashire. The whole economy of the country depended on "the mills".

Today, there are few mills in Lancashire, yet the population has adjusted by absorbing other industries and accepting change. The relatively few remaining textile factories have installed the most modern machinery and replace it every five years or so. The workers have learned new work practices: instead of running four slow looms, they run forty that work ten times faster. Their working week is shorter, their pay is higher, and they have more holidays and recreation. Developing countries have taken over the low-tech textile industry, while developed countries concentrate on higher-tech industries such as electronics and car manufacturing. Furthermore, all these industries have learnt to produce goods and services at a higher quality. Indeed, it was the application of total quality control in Japan in the '50s that made it one of the greatest manufacturing countries in the world.

It is a fallacy that better quality is going to make a product more expensive. The amazing fact is that it works in quite the opposite way. Let me give you an example. A textile mill's weaving department is the hinge on which other departments rely. If the manufacturing quality is poor then threads break and the looms stop. Improving the quality of the product results in less stoppages, less faults and less work for the weavers. As a result, a weaver can operate forty looms rather than ten. Instead of having many inspectors and fixers to fix cloth faults, these are reduced considerably. Whether you are operating a textile mill, an electronics factory or a car plant, reducing the amount of fixes improves efficiency and productivity, producing more items with less staff.

Now that the cloak of secrecy has been lifted from what was once the USSR we can see what happens to a society that does not modernise. Similarly, the difference between East and West Germany was like night and day. Both the USSR and East Germany showed what can happen when a bumbling bureaucracy eliminates two most important aspects of society: *incentive* and *accountability.*

Finally, consider the example of two countries that lost the war but won the peace. Both Germany and Japan emerged from the ruins of their shattered economies with societies that had a collective attitude to succeed. There was no question of resisting change; change was thrust upon them. They emerged from the ruins to enjoy some of the highest standards of living in the world.

Remember how we used to deride cheap Japanese products? We used to say, "Anything can be cheaper if you work for a bowl of rice." Today, the Japanese earn more than we do. Their products are of the highest standards in design, manufacture, quality and reliability. Their success has been generated by productivity.

So what is productivity? It is doing things faster, better, cheaper, with less effort and in less time.

Analysis of work

All work has four individual components:

- Time
- Effort
- Skill
- Method

Each component can be separately identified when an industrial engineer is studying a job function. Let's examine their effect on productivity by taking the first and adding the others, one by one.

Let's say I want a swimming pool installed in my home and I set to do it myself. I get up on Saturday morning and I am in the garden by 8am, leaning my spade and looking at the place where I am going to dig the hole. All day, I lean on the spade and contemplate the hole. At 4.30pm I am still leaning on the spade. I have put in the time, but that is all. I have

45

achieved nothing. For you or me to say, "But I am putting in the time" means nothing unless we add it to the other components.

Instead of leaning on my shovel, I start to dig at 8am. I work fast, furious and hard. At the end of the day I am sweating and exhausted. I think I am going to die. I look at what I have achieved and find a hole. Not a pool hole, but just a hole. The time and the effort I put in is enormous, yet I have achieved very little.

The next day, I hire someone to dig my hole with a front-end loader. He works all day, certainly putting in time but little effort, because he is sitting down flicking levers. In less than a day, there is now a gigantic space for a pool.

When time and effort, represented by me and the spade, were pitted against the method and skill of the front-end loader and the driver, I lost. Granted, you could say that it wouldn't have cost anything if I had dug the hole myself. True, but let's make the comparison equal by asking what it would have cost me to have someone dig my pool hole with a spade against the cost of digging it with the front-end loader. I suggest the machine would have been much cheaper.

This is the application of all the four components: time, effort, skill and method. The difference in productivity is enormous, but the most significant difference is the addition of method.

You begin to work smarter and not harder the moment you ask yourself the critical question, "Is there an easier way of doing this?" This should be applied to every aspect of your life: in the home, the garden and not just at work. How do you think we got mixers and mowers?

If there were a mixed doubles tennis match where Ms. Skill and Mr. Method were playing against Ms. Time and Mr. Effort, the latter would win the game in straight sets. Within yourself, you have to team up with method and develop the skill. Then you will also beat time and effort, hands down.

If I had to allocate points out of 100 to each of the four components of work where 100 equals maximum productivity, I would allocate them as follows:

- Time—1
- Effort—2
- Skill—27
- Method—70

Evolution of systems

The Systems Revolution was the next logical step following the Industrial Revolution. Machines had made the weaving of cloth easier, the drilling of holes quicker and the production of steel less expensive, but it still wasn't good enough. Manufacturers wanted to make production even quicker and cheaper so they could sell more. The stage was set for a new science to be developed and a new actor to emerge.

On stage walked the work-study expert: the industrial engineer. The industrial engineer's job is to study the methods employed in work, develop better ones, train the workers and finally measure the result. This role was further expanded to embrace the organisation of machines and workflow so production lines could work smoothly and efficiently. They were kept operating twenty-four hours a day and far more was produced in the same space with fewer people, greater consistency and lower costs.

Here's an example from a book on the history of industrial engineering. A study was undertaken by a gas company in the USA where men had to shovel mountains of coal as part of the daily operations of the company. I think it's useful to follow this evolution and then relate it to ourselves.

Stage 1: Many men were engaged to shovel coal into sacks. Someone then carried the sacks to a truck where they would be loaded for transportation.

Stage 2: An industrial engineer had men working with different sizes of shovels, from small to very large, in order to determine the optimum shovel size. In other words, what size of shovel filled the most bags with the least effort in

47

Stage 3:
a given time? Once the right shovel was found, everyone was issued with one and productivity increased.

Stage 3: The industrial engineer said to himself, "This is crazy. There has to be an easier way." The firm then engaged an engineering company to design a mechanical shovel and the first front-end loader was developed. Now one man, using a huge scoop, could pick up the coal and drop it into the waiting truck without the need to bag it. This method and newly developed skill replaced the work of many men, who were better employed at less arduous tasks.

Stage 4: Several decades later, another industrial engineer was given the task of improving on what his predecessor had done. He figured that instead of using a front-end loader and truck to take the coal to the ovens, he would use a set of rotating scoops that dropped the coal onto a conveyor, which transported the coal to the waiting trains automatically. Human involvement was purely supervision of the process in the form of a routine check of what was going on. Time and effort had been almost totally eliminated and replaced by method.

Change your approach

Many years ago, when I was thirty, I became Operations Director of quite a large business. My distribution manager, Ivars, was twenty-two. He had joined the company straight from school and worked his way up to this new position. Ivars was dedicated and he put a lot of effort and energy into his job.

One day he came to see me about an increase in pay. I said, "How much do you think you should be earning?" He gave me a figure that was some 50 per cent more than he was currently earning. I then asked, "Why do you believe you deserve so much money?" He replied, "With the responsibility of the job and the enormous hours that I put in, I believe that is what I should be getting."

I leaned forward and looked directly at Ivars and said, "I agree you should be paid that amount but I am not prepared to pay it to you. I have provided the systems for you and your people to work with, yet you continually override the systems and will not insist on the application of a systems discipline from your staff or yourself. You constantly try to by-pass the system or will not maintain it because you are 'too busy'. As a result, everything breaks down and you and your staff have to work twice as hard to make up for it."

Despite years of me pounding systems and discipline into him, he still hadn't learned. I paused for a moment, and then added, "Ivars, I agree with you about what you should be earning but I will not pay it to you until such time as you start to apply the discipline to the system, work smarter and go home at night to enjoy time with your family. Then I will pay you what you ask."

Finally the penny dropped. He left my office, turned his whole approach around and within three weeks, I was happily able to give him a 50 per cent increase in pay. He had finally learned to work smart, not hard, through system and discipline.

The story doesn't end there, as there are other interesting lessons you can learn from his career. Within a year he left the company to take a more responsible position with another firm. I was happy for him because he was meeting the challenge within himself. Six months later he rang me, pleading for me to go around and see him.

The job he had taken was beyond him. The new company didn't have the systems he was used to and the ensuing chaos had almost caused him a nervous breakdown. He was nearly in tears with failure and frustration. At that point, he didn't believe in himself very much, but I did.

A vacancy for a salesman existed in my business and I had him appointed. This was a total change in career, but he applied himself well. He held that position for more than five years then moved on to a more senior selling role with another company. Today, I am proud to say, Ivars is a director of a bigger company than the one we both worked for.

The point is this: his earlier failure did not mean that he was a failure permanently. It simply meant that he had failed at that point in time. Given the right nurturing, given his belief in himself, given some small successes on which he could build bigger successes, he not only conceded his previous failure but grew way beyond it. He hadn't only learned the lesson of 'work smart, not hard', he had undertaken personal development.

Like Ivars, you must change your approach. Don't resist change; waltz with it. Don't accept things the way they are, but make them the way you want them to be. The only person who can change things is you. Have you had ten years' experience or one year's experience repeated ten times?

The person who tries to win with time and effort alone will fail. The person who applies method and skill will win—game, set and match. Don't look to avoid work. Look to make it so easy it isn't a problem. It isn't that you are a poor time manager. The problem is the poor system.

Have you ever wondered why a salesperson can earn over $1 million per year, yet another barely scratches a living? Yet another will totally and utterly fail, leave the job forever and go back to the farm. Let's not look at the failures, however, but at the successes.

Those who succeed rarely put any more time and effort into the job than the unsuccessful. Indeed, you will mostly find they put in less and yet produce a result four or five times greater than the average. If you examined them closely you would find they are putting a great deal of skill into their work, increasing their income exponentially, particularly when plotted against *time* and *effort*.

What you are seeing is the skill factor being added. The more skill you add, the less time and effort is required to achieve the end result. You will note I haven't said *method*. This is because even the top sales producers are not applying method to the degree they should. Once you add method to the equation, income increases even more exponentially but this still does not explain why the majority of people work a working week yet still don't get rich, let alone scale great heights. To get the answer to this, you need to understand and apply *leverage*.

Productivity

Now, here is the deal: YOU DO NOT GET PAID FOR WORK, YOU GET PAID FOR VALUE.

Think not in terms of the time and effort you put in, but instead of the value derived during that time and effort.

In the world today, many senior executives are being paid what is considered an obscene amount of money for doing their job properly. Consider that we all have available to us exactly the same amount of time: 168 hours per week. Deduct from this the need to sleep, say, seven hours a night, which leaves us with 119 hours. Additionally, time needs to be spend on our personal needs, such as eating and personal hygiene, which steals another eighteen hours a week. We also need to commute, which uses another five hours a week. Therefore, we are left with a maximum of ninety-three hours in which to do productive work. Of course, no one can do this without having some leisure time and relationship-building time. As a result, the maximum time a person could effectively spend working is between seventy and eighty hours a week.

Why is it then that some people are paid millions and millions of dollars for working, at most, twice as long as you and I? The only answer is value. They are not paid for the time and effort they put in, but instead the value they produce.

Stop thinking about the work you do. Start thinking of the value that results as a by-product of your work and then you will be on the right track.

Don't major on minors

Not only is it necessary to produce value but it is necessary to work on the things that produce the *greatest* value. People get 'bogged down' too easily. Typically, if a person is faced with a number of tasks they will knock off the easiest ones first. The difficult ones, which invariably produce the greatest value, will be left alone and often forgotten. Learn to guard your time because you have a limited amount of it available to achieve the things you want to achieve. Do not let people waste it, but more importantly make sure *you* are not the guilty party in this respect. There is no one else to blame but yourself if you waste your own time. No one else controls your time but you.

CHAPTER 6

LEVERAGE

Have you ever wondered why people like stock trader Warren Buffet, Bill Gates of Microsoft and Ingvar Kamprad of Ikea were able to come from nothing to become some of the richest men in the world, worth more than $60 billion each? Understand clearly, it is not possible to achieve this huge success simply from personal exertion. There is just not that much time in the world. This kind of success comes from the use of leverage.

We all have the same amount of time available to us, but the variations in people's use of that time is astonishing. First, let's look at the time we have available to achieve what we want to achieve.

Activity	Time/Day	Time/Week
Sleeping	8 hours	56 hours
Eating	2 hours	14 hours
Travelling	1 hour	5 hours
Personal	1.5 hours	10.5 hours
		85.5 hours
Hours available per week		168 hours
		82.5 hours
Hours available for work/leisure		14 hours
Leisure time—say, 2 hours/day		67.5 hours
		38 hours
Work time available		29.5 hours
Normal working week		
Available hours		80 per cent
Percentage of hours above the normal working week		

Working people are often outraged when they hear of senior executives being paid multi-millions of dollars for doing their jobs. Some are paid enormous bonuses simply because the share price has increased. Yet we all have exactly the same time available to us.

You must realise you cannot rely on personal exertion if you wish to achieve great things. You have to take a leaf out of Archimedes book and apply leverage: "Find me a place to stand and I shall move the world".

There are three principal forms of leverage:

People

If you are a tradesman you can obtain leverage by employing other tradesmen and creating work for them. This is the hardest form of leverage because each of those individual tradesmen needs to be highly skilled. So whilst this kind of leverage can achieve success, the success is limited to the person's ability to handle and organise a team of highly-skilled people.

Manufacture, Transport and Retail

Manufacturing is another form of leverage using a combination of people and machinery. A greater result is far easier to achieve using highly productive machinery and fewer skilled people. The drawback, however, is that it requires financial investment and risk.

Leverage via transport is demonstrated by the ability of a single truck driver to move hundreds of tonnes of goods quickly over large distances. Some very wealthy people started in their business with a single truck and went on to build a transport network using good marketing.

Retailing is yet another form of leverage, where goods are be bought from manufacturers and sold to the public.

Property

Property is a commodity that is available to a huge percentage of people, given that property could be the family home. Property ownership is one of the safest and least exertive ways to create wealth, simply because property values will always increase over a period of time.

It is usual these days for a family in the western world to save up and lay down a deposit on a home, which is then bought with a mortgage. Over a period of time the mortgage diminishes while the property increases in value.

Let us say a person buys a home worth $300,000, using a $50,000 deposit and borrowing the remaining $250,000. Because property will usually double in value over a period of seven to ten years, the property after five years is worth $500,000 and the mortgage has been reduced to $220,000. Therefore, the owners' equity has gone from $50,000 to $280,000. That equity can be used to borrow up to 90 per cent of the value of a property package, provided the individual can demonstrate their ability repay the loan. This can also include the rent derived from the investment property. As a result, if that individual bought another investment property worth, say, $400,000, the total value of their property is now $900,000. 90 per cent of this (up to $800,000 of the total property value) can be borrowed.

However, all of that is not necessary. The investor only wants to borrow an additional $400,000, making their totally borrowings $620,000. With the combination of the rent from the new property and the tax deductions due to negative gearing, their mortgage can be further reduced and, in time, more properties can be purchased. When this principle is applied to the commercial property market, the gains can be even greater because the returns are so much better.

Ordinary people can become property millionaires using this method. I know this because I did it myself.

Other forms of leverage

Financial

There are many ways to achieve financial leverage. Money lending, stock market trading and forming investment companies are but a few. I am reliably informed that a bank can loan seven times the value of its deposits.

Therefore, if the bank has $1 billion in deposits, it can achieve with a profit of $7 billion. Of course, this is 'big deal' money lending, but all money lenders start in a small way. Rothchilds started with one branch and build it into an empire.

Entertainment

Clearly, one of the most beneficial forms of leverage is entertainment. Theatre, television, movies and music recordings are just some of the ways of gaining leverage, and this kind of leverage can be spectacularly rewarding. Of course, we can't all be movie stars. Talent is needed, but it is important to note that talent is a totally separate factor from time, effort, skill and method. In most instances, people are born with a talent that can be enhanced by training and practice. However, there are many thousands or even millions of people in the world who have talent in some area, yet do not capitalise on it.

Franchising

The franchise system is a twentieth-century idea that has been triggered by our capacity for mass communication. As a result, two types of franchise have developed.

The first and most powerful form is the brand/product franchise, like McDonalds, which not only promotes their outlets under a common brand but totally controls the preparation, production, packaging and promotion of their products. These businesses have the highest rate of success of any business, as recognised by Michael Gerber in his brilliant book the 'The E Myth'. Gerber noted that 80 per cent of small businesses go broke within the first five years, and 80 per cent of the remaining businesses those go broke in their *next* five years. The secrets of successful franchising are:

- The product must be a USP: a 'Unique Selling Proposition'. There must be no similar product elsewhere. Nowhere is the USP better demonstrated than in the fast food outlets of McDonalds, KFC and Subway.

- The product must be reproduced exactly, each time and every time, no matter where it is produced in the world, to the same standards of taste, cleanliness, organisation and packaging.
- The equipment, organisation and layout must be reproduced at each location, irrespective of the different sites' sizes and shapes.
- The level of service must be not only impeccable, but also as consistent as the product.
- The overall organisation, systems and supply must be consistent to the point of perfection.

Only a limited number of products fit these criteria because they need to be simple and reproducible in spite of high staff turnover. In addition, to keep the costs low and profits high, employees are often in their teens. The whole organisation must be structured so that relatively inexperienced people can be employed and the business can cope with a high turnover of labour.

The second category of franchising is brand franchising, whereby businesses operate under a common brand. Real estate is a very good example of this kind of franchise, whereby a real estate agent will operate under a franchise name, hoping to create business due to name recognition. This kind of franchising has far more limited customer loyalty than a product franchise. However, because of the nature of the business, the franchisor cannot control the level and quality of the product. Each real estate agent has their own personality, and the ability to obtain listings is far more reliant on the personality and ability of the agent than on a controlled product. As a result, there can be little or no consistency in the levels of service provided from one agency to the next.

CHAPTER 7

LEARN TO BE POSITIVE

How do you become a positive person?

It is very simple: you stop being negative. Statistics show 95 per cent of people are negative more often than not. If you don't believe me, come up with a good idea and go to five of your friends and explain it to them. All but one will most likely tell you why it can't be done. Still, they are doing you a favour because now you know some of the things that you must overcome to achieve your dream.

We don't all practice what we preach but, in this department, I do. Let me tell you how I took my first and most significant step to becoming positive. Even the most basic experiences can make a huge difference to your life. I can give you one of my own.

At the age of nine I was at the bottom of the socioeconomic scale in England. My parents were divorced and we lived in what would today be called a slum. Even in comparison to other people in the same environment we were at the bottom of the scale. One day, my brother was invited with some friends to go in a neighbour's car to Blackpool, a seaside resort. I was not invited. From my bedroom window I watched them climb into the car and drive away, filled with self-pity with tears rolling down my cheeks. It was then I realised I had been wallowing in self-pity for years and it was having a very negative effect on my life. To reverse this process I said to myself, "David, there are children in the world who are far worse off than you are. In the third world there are children who are starving, so what are you complaining about?"

This had a very big influence on my life. From then on whenever I felt the pangs of self-pity, I pushed them out of my mind and thought of those children. I didn't realise at the time, but this was my first step down the road of positive thinking that resulted to a massive habit change and a huge move out of my comfort zone. Slowly, I became a positive thinker. Eventually, I projected a positive attitude so profound that if a person wanted to explain something negative, even though it was legitimate, they would apologise to me first.

You can achieve anything you desire, provided you are prepared to have self-discipline and move out of your comfort zone. You must apply the elements of your self-development every day until they become a habit.

Is it hard to do this? Yes, of course it is. Nothing worthwhile comes easy. If it did, everyone would be doing it.

Is it hard work? No. It is simply a matter of making it a habit so that you look at the cup as half full, not half empty.

Will you get it right all the time? Nobody gets it right all the time, but what you achieve will be infinitely greater than if you did nothing.

This too shall pass

Not only will we experience rough roads in our lives but, at some time or another, we will all be faced with tragedy. Some people do not allow themselves to move beyond tragedy and will spend the remainder of their lives in despair. These times are the most serious tests of our ability to 'absorb the punch', to pick ourselves up and get on with life. No matter how tragic the circumstances, it is important to remember that "this too shall pass." This may sound glib, but the reality is that except in a few very rare cases we will eventually get over whatever negatives life deals us. The best thing we can do is to stay busy with the things that interest us.

I cannot think of a more tragic occurrence than the death of a child. Yet, even in this situation, a positive attitude must be pursued after the initial grief. If you hold onto your grief for the rest of your life, you are submitting yourself to a living hell. Of course, there are many occurrences in our lives that are less dramatic than this, yet people seem to hold onto them in an almost masochistic way. Move beyond it—and quickly. Furthermore, don't impose your pain on others. Look upon the circumstances as a test of your ability to be positive and move on.

Don't nurse hurt

Some people seem to take pleasure in remembering, and constantly referring to, hurt they have received. Get over it. Nobody is interested but you. Nursing hurt causes damage only to the person who is doing the nursing, and delight to the person who has caused it. If you want revenge, demonstrate that you are not affected by the hurt someone has caused. Massive success is the best revenge.

Stop feeling sorry for yourself

Self-pity is one of the worst things you can inflict on yourself. We all experience sorrow at one time or another, but the amount you allow it to affect you is directly and proportionately related to the amount of time you allow yourself to feel this way. Not only do you cause damage to yourself, but you damage your relationships with others. People have their own problems; they are often not interested in yours. All you do is make yourself a nuisance to others.

There are many people in the world far worse off than you. Think of them and put your hurt behind you.

Don't be a victim, be a victor

There are many forms of bullying. People of all ages may pick on someone weaker—physically or psychologically—so they can elevate themselves. In all instances, bullies are cowards who, once challenged, will show their true colours. If we are bullied, it is because we allow ourselves to be bullied by not doing anything about it.

Bullies are everywhere. They are in schools, in the workplace, in Government and in families. My advice to you is to fight back, no matter how big and powerful they may appear to be. For example, the Australian Tax

Department once charged me $22,000 in tax and penalties for something I felt was unfair. I challenged them via the legal system. After three years, they paid me back the $22,000 plus a further $11,000 in interest and penalties. Yes, you can even beat the Government if you are in the right. And that is the bottom line: we all have rights and we must stand up for them so that we can become victors rather than victims.

Learn to handle stress

Former Australian Prime Minister Malcolm Fraser once famously said, "Life wasn't meant to be easy." That comment certainly made people sit up and think. Life is filled with difficulties, all of which must be overcome. If we fail to jump the first hurdle, we will stay exactly where we are and probably be dissatisfied with our lot. Life is filled with hurdles to jump, challenges to face. This will not change, but you do have options. You can scale the hurdle, go around it or climb under it. The choice is yours.

Hurdles are annoying and stressful. Stress will occur in your life, as certainly as breathing, but it has to be faced and handled.

Be true to yourself

You can lie to others, but you can't lie to yourself. People who try usually end up being regular guests of our penal systems. The truth is sometimes very difficult, but under no circumstances should you deceive yourself, even if you are successful in deceiving others.

Face the issues you have in life with courage and trust that by addressing these issues you will emerge a positive person.

CHAPTER 8

HANDLING CONFLICT

There is the law and there is justice. They are two separate concepts that have nothing to do with each other. Only occasionally will they coincide. This is because the law has become so complicated that people can get away with murder. The tragedy is that it is getting worse.

If you want proof, consider this: how many times have you heard of people facing the justice system and getting away on a technicality? It is no longer part our judicial system that a person must be proved guilty beyond reasonable doubt. People get away with murder because a minor procedure was done incorrectly by someone in the judicial system. If you don't believe me, consider some of the worst acts of criminal behaviour and tell me: where was the justice?

We only have to look at one continent—Africa—to see some terrible cases of injustice.

- Where is Idi Amin, a man who committed atrocious acts causing deaths of tens of thousands of people, today? He is sitting in a palace in Saudi Arabia, where he has been for decades.
- Where is Gaddafi, who not only sponsored state terrorism, including the Lockerbie Disaster in which he killed hundreds of innocent people? He is now killing more of his own people.
- What has happened to Mubarak of Egypt, who is not only responsible for the deaths of hundreds of protesters but has reportedly stolen $70 billion from his people?

- Where is ex-president Laurent Gbagbo of the Ivory Coast, a man who had thousands of his people killed in a conflict because he refused to relinquish power?
- Where is Mugabe of Zimbabwe who enslaved all his people and turned the bread basket of Africa into a desert?

All over the world, there are people who commit horrendous crimes and get away with it:

- Filipino President Ferdinand stole more than $10 billion from his abjectly poor people
- Adolf Hitler, one of the most evil people in the history of the world, avoided punishment and died at his own hand
- Josef Stalin, who was estimated to be responsible for the deaths of 50 million of his own people in the war, died of natural causes

Never in the history of human conflict has anyone succeeded in the long term. So the question is, "Why do we participate in these conflicts?"

Winning and losing

A conflict will go on until you end it. The simplest and most effective way to achieve this is to give your opponent a small victory. Fagan, in Bryce Courtney's 'The Potato Factory', expressed it slightly differently. He said "Always leave a little bit on the plate."

The most dangerous conflict in the history of the world was the Cuban Missile Crisis. It is also a dramatic example of giving the other side a win. Though most people are aware that the Russians withdrew, few understand the true situation. To bring about the Russians' appeasement, Kennedy wisely agreed to withdraw all missiles from Turkey. All of these missiles were outdated; the latest ICBMs were able to reach Russia from the mainland of the United States. Kennedy gave a little, but that concession allowed Khrushchev to save face by giving him a win.

If Kennedy could achieve this in front of a world audience, we should be able to do the same on our own small scale. To win a war often we have to lose a skirmish or even a battle. What matters is the win. How do we do this? Simply, by making some small concession that may be irrelevant to the larger issue but that makes your opponent feel they have not lost everything.

Whenever I hear a person engaged in conflict say, "It is the principle of the thing," I know there are going to be two losers. This often occurs in divorces where one side demands something that is not valuable in comparison to the total amount being claimed, yet will spend thousands of dollars in lawyers' fees to get it. Always remember, the only beneficiaries from these conflicts are the lawyers, who stretch the conflict as far as they can.

The United States is the major power in the world today, but, like most high achievers, it has become a victim of 'tall poppy syndrome'. In fact, if you added the military spending of every other country in the world it still would not equal that of the USA. I ask you this: "When has the United States fought a war of conquest so as to take that land and those people as its own?" Alaska was purchased from Russia. A large swath of land was acquired from France in the Louisiana Purchase. Many islands, such as Hawaii, are now part of the United States today because they asked—nay, begged—to be.

Certainly, they have fought wars that could (and should) be judged as regrettable, such as Vietnam. Other than that, their participation has been either under the auspices of the United Nations or NATO. We should be thankful that the dominant power in the world today is reluctant to engage in international conflict. Nowhere is this highlighted more clearly than in the Libyan conflict, when the United States insisted on a back seat and pushed France and Britain to the forefront.

So, what is this leading to? It is this: "Fight the battles you can win." Furthermore, avoid going headlong into conflict because of the "principle of the thing". Work out what is worth fighting for *before* you fight.

I offer you this as an example from my own life. When my ex-wife and I decided to divorce in 1999, we had a very complicated set of issues both emotionally and financially. Before discussing a solution, we both agreed to put our two children first to minimise any harm the divorce might cause them. We decided to live in the same house, using separate bedrooms. There was very rarely any conflict. Financially, we worked out a fair deal for both of us and went to our lawyer together to have him approve this agreement with the courts. In other words, we did not go into our separate corners and fight.

Instead of this costing us $50,000 each, the cost was $3,600 in total. But more importantly, Liz and I are very good friends today and I will always do whatever I can to assist her. For me, the greatest reward came many years later, when my youngest daughter Sian said to me, "Dad, apart from the initial shock of you announcing you were going to separate, I can honestly tell you that neither Che nor I have ever had the slightest problem emotionally with your divorce. In fact, we have gained a wonderful stepfather and a fantastic stepmother."

There are two steps you can take to overcome difficult situations.

See the other person's point of view

This is sometimes a very difficult task. It involves putting your own feelings and point of view aside for a moment whilst you examine the other person's case. There is no situation where one person is 100 per cent right and another is 100 per cent wrong. Whatever the balance, there is always right and wrong on both sides. For you to be able to see another's point of view, you must display great strength of character. A wonderful by-product of this is a sense of peace that gives you strength. It is rather like the idea of Catholic confession, which allows a person to unburden themselves and remove a great weight from their conscience.

It never fails to amaze me while watching real life court cases how often a person who is absolutely guilty over something quite minor will defend themselves to the death with ridiculous logic. It takes a very strong person to stand up and say they are right. However, it takes an even stronger person to admit they are wrong.

Seek mediation

For me, mediation is rarely the answer but for many it is essential. For mediation to work, your choice of a mediator is critical. A mediator must be unscrupulously neutral; even the slightest indication that they are favouring one side will cause the mediation to break down. Of course, this is extremely difficult, simply because people will often cling to their point of view without seeing the other side of the argument. For you, I offer the following points:

- Actively listen. Have an open mind to what is being said. Try to understand that they, too, have a point of view.
- Accept responsibility. In the areas of your relationship where you have done the wrong thing, accept it and stop trying to defend it. Make it very clear that you are acknowledging that point.
- Be as detached and clinical as possible. Being over-emotional will blind you and stop you from finding a solution.
- Understand that the outcome you desire is to *achieve a solution*. If this point of view were taken at all times by all parties, 90 per cent of conflict would be resolved immediately.
- Be prepared to accept criticism.
- Don't blame. This goal is to find solutions, noy allocate blame or get revenge.
- Don't hang onto your story. Everybody tells themselves stories, but they are often used to justify the way they feel. Get over your story. Put it behind you and move on.

So what is the bottom line?

- Conflict can only be created with two or more people.
- Do not look for revenge. Look for solutions.
- Do not think only of the effect it has on you, but also take into account the effect it has on your loved ones.
- Finally, "Losers fight, winners fly over the top."

CHAPTER 9

LEADERSHIP

Whether leaders are born or created is a matter for dispute. Certainly, some are born with leadership qualities whilst others developed them as they progress through life. The reality is that most people take on a leadership role when raising their family. Of course, not everyone is qualified for this role; poor leadership within a family often results in unruly children who become even more unruly adults.

You do not only have to the head of a nation or an organisation to be a leader. Certainly, those people do possess leadership qualities, but leadership is present at all levels and stratas of society. This is best demonstrated in the workplace whenever an individual without title or tribute seizes the initiative to lead his fellow workers.

Furthermore, it is not necessary to be a leader to 'Unlock the Giant Within' because "giants" can develop many qualities and have many successes which do not necessarily qualify them to be leaders. That direction is a personal matter; you can go wherever you choose. If you do choose a leadership direction, there are rules which you need to follow.

1.   The Rules of Leadership

A leader is more important than an organisation

For almost 1,500 years, Rome was one of the greatest empires the world has known. The single greatest reason for its success was the organisation of a standing army. Throughout the entire life of the empire, its organisational structure was, under normal circumstances, unbeatable. Indeed, on many occasions it defeated a much larger force. Yet, sometimes it *was* defeated. Why is this so? Because no matter how strong an organisation and structure may be, it is still dependent on a leader.

No one displayed this principle more dramatically than Julius Caesar. Throughout his entire career, Caesar never lost a battle. He never asked any man to do something he was not prepared to do himself. For example, when marching through the Alps, he was in the front line, digging through the snow with his men. A similar display of leadership was also evidenced in World War 2 during Montgomery's defeat of Rommel in the western desert, where Montgomery assisted his generals at the front line, despite almost being captured at one point. If you want you people to surge forward, you must lead them from the front line, not the rear.

A leader must set standards and disciplines

Your people must understand the roles they have to play within the organisation. They need to clearly understand what is expected of them and why. Having outlined that, you can then set standards for both performance and quality. These standards must be high or you will only achieve mediocrity. Remember, the higher you aim, the higher your final target will be.

In the '50s, Japan was a nation recovering from the devastation of war. In those days, labour was not only cheap, but workers were highly educated, intelligent and disciplined. The Samurai code was by no means extinguished by war. Japan began producing manufactured goods, which, at the time, were considered inferior to European products. At once stage, they even named a Japanese town 'Sheffield' so they could make cutlery with 'Made in Sheffield' imprinted on it. Of course, it is an entirely different matter today. Japanese products are considered amongst the best in the world and the standard of living in Japan is extremely high. This turn-around was brought about by setting standards and implanting disciplines.

Always be positive

You cannot be a negative leader. Have you ever noticed how we avoid negative people and are drawn to the positive? A leader is there to inspire, but a negative person cannot possibly achieve that. What Martin Peter said is largely true: people who show promise get promoted and, at some stage, overreach their capabilities. This is rarely for technical reasons. Mostly it is because they have overreached their leadership potential at that point in time.

If you have doubts or think negatively, your goals will be impossible to meet. Success is infectious; doubt is contagious. When things go wrong, look closely at what did not work and fix it, because repeating failure is only going to lead to even more failure.

2. When placed in command:

Take charge and have strength

You cannot be strong for others unless you are strong for yourself. No matter how selfish this sounds, it is a reality. For example, say you lived in a third-world country and there was not enough food to sustain your whole family. Seemingly unselfish parents would give food to their children and go without themselves. This would very quickly lead to a situation where the parents became so weak from hunger they could not support their family. In those circumstances, it is better for the breadwinner to maintain his or her strength so that they could work to sustain the family and keep them all alive.

At all times, be firm but fair. You cannot be soft or unfair, but you must have a no-nonsense approach which is clearly signaled and understood. Your motto should be, "This is the way we do things around here."

As a leader you must accept reason but never tolerate a threat. With the little things, you can apply the saying, "Losers fight, winners fly over the top," but dealing with a threat is an entirely different matter. It must be met with all the 'fight', skill and energy you possess.

You must be strong, yet flexible. This is by no means a contradiction. For example, in earthquake zones like Japan and California, skyscrapers are built with flexibility so in the event an earthquake strikes they can bend like straw in the wind rather than break and collapse. You cannot afford to be rigid or allow pride stand in the way of good sense.

Always lead by example. Do not expect others to do something that you are not prepared to do yourself. Always remember, you need respect, not popularity. If you want to be a captain, mould yourself on a great one. Do not be Captain Smith, who was too lax, or Captain Bligh, who was too tough, but Captain Cook, who took himself and his men around the world on three missions and brought them back safely. He insisted his men ate sauerkraut, even although they hated it. As a result, there was never a case of scurvy on his ship.

Be a leader, not a manager

A leader is a person who has good management capabilities but is also entrepreneurial. Managers and leaders are not the same. Leadership is to a great extent personality within a person, which is only 15 per cent technical and 85 per cent skill. If you need more information, read "The E Myth" by Michael Gerber. Great managers do not necessarily make good leaders. In fact often, they make bad leaders. The Peter Principle states, "A person is promoted to their level of incompetence and there they stay."

Be proactive

You must clearly understand the vast difference between being *pro*active and being *re*active. Having a plan is being proactive. Furthermore, having a plan that takes into account all the things that could go wrong is superbly proactive. Being reactive means you react to something that is not part of the plan. As a result, you must learn to sense an oncoming situation. As I mentioned previously, the most wonderful thing about not planning is that failure comes as a total surprise and is not preceded by long periods of doubt, worry and depression.

You do not have to work harder; you simply have to work smarter. Your situation and organisation is a small part of that. By creating a plan to cover *all* situations you can apply 'management by exception', which means handling the exceptional when it occurs. Because you have been proactive, you have given yourself the time to deal with it properly. In all of this, your judgment is critical.

Deal with the Gorilla

In most organisations there is a person who thinks so highly of themselves that they become extremely disruptive to the rest of the team. The 900 pound Gorilla usually, this person is unfortunately one of the better performers and seeks to terrorise those they think are not up to their level. Furthermore, because they are often the top performer, they believe themselves irreplaceable. They are not. The first step you must take is to dismiss your fear of losing them. Indeed, unless you deal with them, you will lose the rest of your team either through resignations or poor performance. No one person is more important than the team as a whole, not even you.

At the opposite end of the scale, there is a person who I call the '900 pound Organ Grinder's Monkey'. This person dances and prances around with a cup, collecting pennies, whilst you grind away and play a tune on the organ. If they cannot keep up to par, they lose their place on the team.

But the worst of all is the '900-pound Organ Grinder's Monkey'. These people are not just poor performers but see themselves as big performers and are extremely disruptive. Your team can do without them.

Accept responsibility

You will always have problems. Furthermore, once you have solved those problems, another set will arise. Confront the issues, don't shirk them. Find solutions, because for every problem there *is* a solution. Above all else, don't buckle under criticism.

Please note: Accepting responsibility is not simply a matter of apologising to others. Admit responsibility to yourself, and accept it. Everybody makes mistakes—you will continue with that habit during your lifetime. If you don't, you will just sit on your hands and do nothing. It is only by taking and accepting responsibility to yourself that you can grow. There are times when you will be hurt, not just by colleagues but also friends and family. Don't nurse hurts. Confront the situation and move on.

3. A leader must:

Be strong

As I pointed out earlier, you can only be strong for others if you are strong for yourself. A lifesaver trying to save a drowning man will often have to dunk them under water to control them. Do the same yourself. Be decisive, especially when you are wrong and you need to change your decision. Allow people to grow because you can only move ahead when you have someone capable to replace you. Allow people to use their initiative, but in a controlled manner. At all times, provide clear direction and boundaries. If there is a series of tasks that must be faced, do the hard things first. The bottom line is that you must face the issues.

The two most important things you must give your children are love and discipline.

You can give too much of anything: too much money, too much attention, too much adoration. One thing you can never give a child too much of is love. Even if you did, the worst that would happen is that the child would feel even more secure.

A child also needs discipline. I don't mean harshness, but setting boundaries and recognising 'no-go zones'. Throughout their lives, a child will test your love for them by doing things they should not. If you allow this to go on unchecked, they will invariably end up being spoilt and unpopular. Apply the same philosophy in your organisation.

Allow mistakes

This seems to be one of the most difficult ideas for people to learn and accept: no one is perfect and everyone makes mistakes. But people should not make the same mistake twice. Allow them to use their initiative. You cannot give responsibility without giving the corresponding authority. In doing so, you are allowing a person to make mistakes.

Every time you gamble and lose, it could be said that you made a mistake. If you win 51 per cent of the time you are a winner, even though you made mistakes 49 per cent of the time. The question is whether you allow other people to make 49 per cent mistakes. The answer to that is invariably, "No." It is therefore a question of allowable mistakes.

What percentage of mistakes would you allow? How much damage needs to be made with a single mistake for it not to be allowable? Of course, these questions are very judgmental, but the bottom line is how much a person learns from the mistakes they have made because unless a person changes the habit of that mistake it will get repeated.

Learn to understand the difference between mistakes and failure. Mistakes can be corrected, but failure is fatal.

Be credible

To be credible you must always mean—and do—what you say. This, of course, sets a high standard. Only make threats if you are prepared to carry them out. Only stand in judgment if you think you are right. Avoid doing or saying something that you are not prepared to back up. If you act, then recognise you were wrong, admit it and change your decision.

4. Be demanding

All leaders are demanding of others. Mother Teresa, in doing her saintly work, was as demanding of her followers as she was of herself. This is a mark of leadership. Don't demand something from others you are not prepared to do yourself. A failure to do this will not only compromise your credibility, but will also lose you respect.

At one point, part of Julius Caesar's army mutinied. After he quelled the mutiny, he brought all his soldiers in front of him and simply said, "You are no longer my boys." The hardened warriors were in tears. You are not a leader just because you were appointed you have to earn it by demonstrating your skills and winning their love and trust.

Give recognition

You can only be demanding if you also give recognition. Remember, money is not everything. In war, people will risk and even lose their lives for their mates and a medal. In normal life, it is very demotivating if a person works hard and does not receive recognition for the work they have done. After all, a few words cost nothing; even you only say, "Good job," you are encouraging that person to do better. If someone works without any recognition at all they may think they are not doing well. In fact, this can often cause them to perform more poorly. Some managers mistakenly think that if they say nothing their staff will try to do better. In the majority of cases, this is not so.

Be decisive

I have identified three key decision-making styles:

- The 'cover your butt' style, where everything is put into writing. Less is achieved because the mechanics of doing this takes too much time.
- The analysis and evaluation style, where the result is so certain that it cannot be wrong. This, of course, takes an even greater amount of time and is typical of the style used in Government and industry. By the time an irrefutable conclusion is reached, something else is available and the analysis is required all over again.
- Caesar's style, where you collect information as quickly as possible, formulate a plan and make a decision. Just as importantly, you make the necessary adjustments as events unfold.

Remember to "make a decision, because even a wrong decision is better than no decision at all."

CHAPTER 10

My Proverbial Collection

Over the years, I have assembled all the sayings which have been related to me and which I feel hold an enormous amount of truth. I have written them down in my collection. I wish to share them with you; perhaps some will find their way into your Proverbial Collection.

Many have been used in this book, but I will repeat them here, if only because there is a fine line between repetition and reinforcement. In most cases, I'll relate what the idea means to me. Whilst if may seem that I am stating the obvious, I have learned never to assume that my interpretation is the only one, or that the way I see things is the way everyone sees things.

YOU CAN'T BE A LITTLE BIT PREGNANT!

There are certain times in life when you must decide 'to be or not to be'. You are or you are not, you do or you do not. Many of us want to take only the bits we personally want, without accepting the parts we don't like. With some things that is possible, but with others it isn't.

THERE IS NO SUCH WORD AS CAN'T!

Isn't it astonishing what people have achieved in the last 100 years? Consider the number of things that can't be done that have suddenly become a part of everyday life.

MASSIVE ACTION GETS MASSIVE RESULTS!

The result is always in proportion to the action taken. If you are not happy with a portion of your life, then take action on it. No action means no result. Some action means some results. Massive action means massive results.

PLEASE, ONE MORE BOOM!

The real estate agent's lament: 'Oh, please God, give me just one more boom and I promise not to waste it next time'.

TRIED THAT, DIDN'T WORK!

If the human race had been put off by the number of times we have tried and failed, we would still be rubbing sticks together in caves. Joe Braysich once demonstrated to me what *tried* means. He said, 'Try to get out of that chair'. I immediately stood up. He said, 'No! Sit down and try to get out of the chair'. I then understood what he meant. I sat there and struggled, without my bottom leaving the seat. That is trying: getting nowhere.

How many people tried to fly before the Wright brothers succeeded? How many people tried to make a steam engine before James Watt succeeded? How many people have tried to sell before they succeeded?

WE DO NOT KEEP AND FEED HOLY COWS!

Whilst there are things in my life which are sacred, I always allow myself the right to revise my view. Certainly, I will never hold sacred something which will harm my family, or anyone else for that matter.

INCOME DOES NOT FAR EXCEED PERSONAL DEVELOPMENT!

Don't wait for someone to give you something. Force them to give it to you because you deserve it. The only way you will earn more is by going to work on yourself.

MAN WILL NEVER FLY!

Do you want to bet?

IS IT HALF-FULL OR IS IT HALF-EMPLY?

This represents two different views of the same situation. The half-full is the positive view of the situation and the half-emp.ly is the negative view of the same situation. Your view of any situation is determined by your positive or negative attitude.

DON'T GO AWAY UNHAPPY, JUST GO AWAY!

You can make some of the people happy some of the time, you may make most of the people happy most of the time, but you can't make all of the people happy all of the time.

I AM IRREPLACEABLE!

If you ever think you are irreplaceable, I suggest you get a bucket and pour water in it until it is three-quarters full. Roll up your sleeve and stick in your hand. Pull it out and have a look at the hole you have left.

DON'T BE A NINE HUNDRED POUND GORILLA!

Nine hundred pound gorillas are the successful people in your environment who are so conceited that they think they are irreplaceable. It is an object in their lives to terrorize everyone around, or be at least extremely disruptive.

My advice to anyone who employs a nine hundred pound gorilla is to get rid of it and watch your business prosper. In every case where this has been done, the business has been far better off.

Don't become a nine hundred pound gorilla!

DON'T BE AN ORGAN GRINDER'S MONKEY!

At the opposite extreme to the nine hundred pound gorilla is the organ grinder's monkey. Whilst the owner grinds away at the organ handle day after day, the monkey dances and prances around collecting pennies.

I use to identify the monkeys and the gorillas as being two extremes in a sales office, until I discovered there was a third dimension, which is the worst of all: a nine hundred pound organ grinder's monkey.

IF IT'S NOT BROKEN, DON'T FIX IT!

This can mean a lot of things. I can mean that if something is working well, leave it alone and put your energy and attention into something more important. On the other hand, it can be an excuse for not moving with the times, in which case it would be more appropriate to say, 'If it's not broken, break it'. Both of these are probably extremes. My attitude is: Don't wait till it breaks; maintain and improve it.

CHANGE IT THREE TIMES!

Whenever you develop or introduce something new, it's never right until you've changed it at least three times. This not only reflects an attitude that accepts change, but an open-minded attitude that develops the changes.

DEVELOPMENT MEANS CONSTANT CHANGE!

The most successful car in the world was the Volkswagen Beetle, which stayed in production for over three decades. From the tens of thousands of parts and components constituting the original design, only seven remain unchanged.

IF YOU BELIEVE IT WORKS, IT WORKS!

You will never make anything work if you don't believe in it. Belief is therefore a self-fulfilling prophecy.

"NO" IS SAFE!

No does not mean total rejection, but more often means, 'I have doubts, therefore my answer must be No'. Conversely, Yes means commitment and responsibility. You will find that managers and executives who lack competence are very quick to say No. You will also find that many clients who say No really mean, 'I still have doubts; you haven't convinced me yet'.

A SENSE OF URGENCY!

All successful people have a sense of urgency about life, work and about life's work. A person without a sense of urgency is destined to mediocrity.

IT IS BETTER TO TRY AND FAIL, THAN FAIL TO TRY!

Don't remain in the crowd, shouting advice and abuse from the safety of the sidelines. If you want to be in life, then join the team and start to play.

CRISIS MANAGEMENT!

If you really want to work hard and not smart, practice crisis management. If you find yourself constantly putting out bushfires, running from one crisis to another, you are practicing crisis management. Lots of people practice it so much that they do nothing else.

MANAGEMENT BY NO SURPRISES!

This is taking a more advanced approach by being proactive in your management. Organise your thinking so that you anticipate the problem. Defensive driving is the only way to avoid accidents.

MANAGEMENT BY EXCEPTION!

If you and your business are organized, then you are able to practice management by exception. There is no way that you can organize everything to avoid the unexpected. It will happen. If you have your business organized, you are able to handle the unexpected, and therefore practice management by exception.

SERVICE TO DEATH!

Service your clients so well that you eliminate the need to sell yourself, as your clients will sell you, for you.

DON'T THROW THE BABY OUT WITH THE BATH WATER!

Development means a process of constant improvement, it does not mean getting rid of everything and starting all over again.

HAVE A HEALTHY EGO!

Everyone has an ego. Not everyone has an ego problem. A healthy ego is vitally important to you, whereas an unhealthy ego will eventually destroy you.

' YOU KNOW ME!'

What a brilliant overstatement. I don't even know myself that well, never mind someone else. Anyone making that statement is making a huge assumption. Let me tell you what ASS-U-ME means: it makes an ass out of you and me.

TAKE A CUSTOMER PERSPECTIVE!

I will say no more.

IT'S RISKY!

I'll tell you how risky life is: you'll never get out of it alive.

LOSERS FIGHT, WINNERS FLY OVER THE TOP!

All the successful senior executives I have worked with and respect have inner strength and conviction. But they don't get bogged down fighting matters they cannot win, irrespective of whether it is relevant or irrelevant.

THEY'LL LET ME KNOW!

If you even think that the customers are going to get in touch with you when they are ready, you are dead in the water.

FEAR IS THE ENEERGY WHEN I DO MY BEST WORK!

Ordinary feelings develop ordinary work. Extraordinary feelings develop extraordinary work. Powerful feelings develop powerful work.

YOU CHOOSE!

The most powerful sates and management expression is 'You choose!'. Even in a conflict, in fact particularly in a conflict, the 'You choose' method works brilliantly. For example, 'You either do it this way, or work for someone else. You choose!'. Or 'Which marketing program do you wish to choose?'.

DO IT NOW!

If you have decided to do something, do it now or I guarantee it will not be done. At the very least, if you have any intention of doing it, write it on your To Do list.

ASK!

The first step in getting what you want is to ask. That doesn't guarantee you will get it, because you may not have asked in the right way or often enough. But the starting point is to ask.

THE CUSTOMER IS ALWAYS RIGHT!

The customer is not always right, but the customer's feelings should always be treated with the utmost respect.

YOUR ATTITUDE DETERMINES YOUR ALTITUDE!

Your income or position in life has little to do with your background or education, but a lot to do with your attitude.

CHAPTER II

ABOUT THE AUTHOR

David Pilling was a war baby born on 31 January, 1943, in St Mary's Hospital, Manchester. His family lived in a council house where his mother and grandmother sewed shoes whilst his father was at war.

When David was five years old, his family moved to a town called Nelson. Shortly afterwards, his parents divorced, which, in those days, was a rare and strange occurrence.

His mother, grandmother and brother moved to another terraced house on a dirt road in a slum area, situated across from a foundry and engineering works. It was, of course, necessary for his mother to work, so David and his brother were left to cope as best they could. This meant walking to and from school, enviously watching other children riding their bikes and enjoying a stable family life. There was little fun or pleasure in their lives, and certainly no holidays. On one occasion, when David fell and dirtied his best suit, his mother beat him to the floor in a fit of rage, and proceeded to kick him as he tried to protect himself under a table.

When he was ten, his mother met the man who was to become his step-father. This man was also a divorcee with a son. Out of wedlock, they had David's half sister, Angela. She was a beautiful baby and David loved her dearly, taking care of her so often that she called him "Mummy". David's dedication to his sister detracted from his schooling, as he was often taken out of class to look after his sister while his mother and step-father worked. Despite this, David was a top student throughout junior school and was only surpassed in his class by two girls, both of whom were quite brilliant.

In the 1950s English education system, eleven-year-old students were required to take a test called 'The Eleven Plus', which determined which strata of school you were permitted to attend. At the top were the Grammar Schools, in the middle were Technical Schools and at the bottom were the Secondary Moderns. David failed his 'Eleven Plus' and was subsequently sent to a Secondary Modern. The best hope he had upon graduating from these schools was to become a tradesman.

Even for poor slum dwellers, David's family were at the bottom of the pile. At the age of twelve, he got a before-school job delivering milk to local households, rising at 5.30 every morning and working until he was dropped off at school, without breakfast, at 9am. Rain was the standard weather in Lancashire during spring, summer and autumn. But during the snowy winter months, the weather became so cold that the milk in the van would freeze until it expanded, forming a frozen tube that popped out of the bottle with a silver or gold cap sitting on the top. After three hours of this exposure every morning David was dropped off at school, wet through. He dripped through class. The school provided a free three course lunch which was often his only substantial meal of the day.

People living in this environment could not help but develop a disease of attitude which kept them slotted into life at the bottom of the food chain. David's expectations and ambitions were very limited. In this lowest tier of British education, students were allowed to leave school at the end of the term after your fifteenth birthday. In April, 1958, David left school and took a job as a labourer in a textile mill. The following year, desperate to achieve some status and wanting to experience the glamour of travel, he joined the merchant navy as a steward.

After two voyages through some of the worst trouble spots in the Mediterranean, including war-torn Cyprus, Israel and Algeria, David had had enough 'glamour' to last a lifetime. He returned to England where he visited the local Labour Exchange and tried to find a job. This was a notable moment in his life. The interviewer asked him, "How good are your maths, English and spelling?" David replied, "Good, OK, and terrible." Much to his surprise, he was offered a job as a design office assistant in one of the local textile mills. This unbelievable opportunity was only offered because, at the time, nobody wanted a job in the Lancashire textile industry as it was thought to be dying. But for David, this job meant status and opportunity, so he took the job.

Every person has moments of significance in their lives, and David was soon to experience one. He started his new job on a Monday, and quickly found he was out of his depth. Walking to work on Wednesday, he had severe doubts about his ability to cope with his job. He felt very much like as though he were drowning. However, on that Wednesday morning, walking down the street towards his work, David said to himself, "This is your opportunity. Don't let it slip through your fingers. Be resolved." For the first (but certainly not the last) time in his life, David moved out of his comfort zone and took his first step down the road to self-improvement and success.

Fortunately, David worked for a very nice man called Arthur Stevenson who took him under his wing and helped him deal with this discomfort. Given the economic climate at the time, it came as no surprise that the company was closed down after a Government reorganisation of the textile industry. David was offered another job with another company in the same building. It was a small business with only the owner working in the office. David acted as his 'sidekick'. Whilst the pay was very low, the experience could not have been better. He learnt payroll administration, costings and organisation. He learnt to weave and design, and was involved with every aspect of the textile mill. Two of the weavers, Aunty Nina and Aunty Gladys, took him under their wings and gave him the mothering at work that he did not receive at home, for which he was immensely grateful. David thrived in this environment and enjoyed the privileged position of being the only "boy" in the company.

After two and a half years, David saw a job advertisement for an assistant designer with one of the biggest and most prestigious textile companies in the area. He applied successfully for the position and entered a new world. His office was on the ground floor of a large, prominent house with its own gardens. The office, which he shared with the designer Arthur Hanson, was beautifully decorated. This gave David his first taste of a world outside his own. Arthur was very kind to him and became a life-long friend.

In 1963, his mother and stepfather, disillusioned with the British working class system, decided to move to Australia under the Assisted Immigration Scheme. David was placed in a position where he had to choose between staying in England with an enjoyable and secure job without a family and venturing into the great unknown with his family. He chose the latter and never regretted his decision. His family moved to Adelaide where, at the time, there were only three textile companies. He successfully gained employment with the largest, ACTIL.

There were no design opportunities as the company only produced white sheets but based on his textile experience David was given a job in the technical department, which involved quality control, industrial engineering and production planning. This gave him access to all aspects of the company's vertical operations, from raw cotton at one end to packaged, manufactured goods at the other. David taught himself industrial engineering, quality control and production planning on the job. He then learnt sophisticated financial analysis and costings on the processes and machinery later being installed in the plant. Despite his poor education, David had a natural flair for all aspects of the organisation and quickly grasped the fundamentals and intricacies of sophisticated production management. Unfortunately, there was little opportunity for progress within the company and his work went unappreciated. As a result, after eight years he applied for and obtained a position at a new textile company in Melbourne. This event marked the beginning of one of the most difficult, yet productive, periods of David's life, and the commencement of his real personal development.

On moving to Melbourne, David found he was gravely under qualified for his new position. A new textile mill had to be built, the machinery installed, infrastructure and systems to be established, staff employed, costings done, marketing, sales and distribution to be instituted, and accounting and administration developed—all from the ground up.

After three months on the job, the enormity of the task that lay ahead began to dawn on him. David started to have sleepless nights and the beginnings of a nervous breakdown. He went to a doctor who gave him medication and said, "These pills will not solve your problems, but will help you see them more clearly." It is a lesson we should all learn: when the going gets tough, seek help.

Even before the building was finished, occupation commenced with a delivery of machinery which required assembly and erection. David's first office was a desk on top of a pile of packing crates from which he directed workers on the installation. He also assisted with these tasks so he could learn and pass on this knowledge. Things took shape slowly, but every part was a new challenge. David learned to operate new machines and held the organisation together whilst the owner worked on sales and marketing.

After six months, David's nerves were shattered and he was ready to throw in the towel. But then he remembered that fateful Wednesday morning, years before, and reached inside himself to find the resolve to continue. He stayed with the company. Six months later the mill began producing goods and the first distribution commenced.

For the next two years David worked twelve hours a day, seven days a week. He sometimes worked through the night and on one occasion did not go home for three days because of the pressure of work. However, the business was successful and David was eventually appointed Operations Director. In this role, he was responsible for almost every aspect of the business, including manufacturing, office administration, accounting and New Zealand export.

After four years, it was clear that industry trends were changing and woven bedspreads represented a diminishing market. As a result, the company began searching the world for other products that could be manufactured and distributed. This formed a very significant part of David's experience.

Within several years he had organised the manufacture of twenty seven different products in various parts of the world, each involving great complexity in planning. For one product alone required velvet woven and hand-screen printed into twenty seven different patterns, cut into squares and patchworked in India. The fabric was then shipped to South Korea, through Japan, to be hand-quilted and constructed into the finished bedspread, and finally shipped to Australia.

During this time, he spent four months a year travelling overseas, staying an average of 36 hours at each destination. His main objective was to find and source products which he could duplicate at low cost before bringing an excellently priced, quality product to Australia.

At about this time, the owner of the business had a disagreement with his South African partners and organised a buy-out, with key employees given the opportunity to become shareholders. David became the second-highest shareholder after buying 20 per cent of the business. Although the pressure was enormous, David's life was very exciting and he experienced tremendous personal growth in terms of both development and experience.

During 1979, the major shareholder developed a business plan to expand the business into the sheeting area. David costed a number of versions, projecting their feasibility at various levels of sales. At the time, the business was creating $6 million worth of sales and a profit above 15 per cent. His projections showed that this expansion would need to produce $11.2 million worth of sales just to break even. He called a shareholders' meeting and the plan was put to the vote. David was outvoted by all shareholders and the plan went ahead against his wishes.

January of 1981 marked the start of David's roughest road. He separated from his first wife, Carol, but maintained good relationships with her and his children. Shortly afterwards, Carol met her husband-to-be, with whom she wanted to buy their former family home. Unfortunately, David had to inform them that the home was not only mortgaged but guaranteed against the company's loans. He told them, "I believe that in 18 months' time I will be going broke and I don't want to drag you and the kids down with me. Let us arrange a legal settlement and I will somehow find the money so you can separate your affairs from mine."

Sure enough, 18 months later the company went into receivership, causing David a total loss of his wealth. The company was bought out by a large textile company, but David was broke. In February, 1982 he suffered a major heart attack and underwent quadruple by-pass surgery. During this time, he also suffered a total nervous breakdown for which he was admitted to hospital and put on medication. To add insult to injury, he was fired by the new company as they considered him surplus to requirements. This was the lowest down point in his life.

Fortunately, his old employer, ACTIL, hired David for two weeks as a consultant to style their bedspread range. This was a major turning point. He not only completed his task but recognised that this company, in spite of its size, had no design or styling direction. With the help of the design staff he put together story boards of designs to be considered for future development. He was immediately offered a five month contract to develop these ideas.

The range he launched five months later more than doubled the company's sales record. As a result, he was offered the position of Design Director, which he gratefully accepted. David entered one of the most productive and happiest times in his life. This is absolute proof that you can achieve anything you set your mind to.

Within a year, the company was taken over by another group whose management style David did not agree with, and he left to become General Manager of a clothing company.

The year was 1987. The Australian Government's plan for the textile industry was to remove all protection by 1994. This was the death knell for textiles manufacturing in Australia, so David looked outside the industry for the first time in almost thirty years. It was a daunting task. To take on and learn a new industry at the age of forty-five was difficult enough but he could not afford to start at the bottom and work his way up. He was desperate to maintain his income level.

In August 1988, he was appointed CEO of The Professionals Real Estate Group in South Australia, a group of twenty-eight semi-franchised offices. The Board of Directors hired David because he had marketing and management experience. He knew nothing about real estate, but they saw this as an advantage. They did not want another real estate agent to tell them what they already knew; they wanted someone with a different kind of expertise to show them what they did not know. This move was hugely successful and propelled David into a new professional world.

During the three and a half years he was with The Professionals, David increased their market share from 6 per cent to a massive 18 per cent. More importantly, his responsibility for hundreds of sales consultants led him to discover a talent for leadership. Unfortunately, by 1992 his heart condition had grown steadily worse as his original bypasses continued to block. As a result, David decided to change his lifestyle and launch himself onto the speaking circuit as a trainer in real estate.

He wrote six magazine articles, called 'The Dynamics of the '90s', which were widely published throughout Australia and New Zealand. Furthermore, he was invited to write two books to be published for the industry; one on Sales and Marketing and the other on Management. During this incredibly happy period in his life, he spent six months writing his books which, when published, became industry best-sellers. On the basis of this success, he was able to legitimately launch his speaking career.

David's seminars were incredibly successful. At each session he would speak to up to 300 people who had paid $600 for a two-day seminar. These were conducted regularly throughout Australia and New Zealand and occasionally in the USA and UK. David invested his earnings into commercial real estate.

During this time, David was constantly battling his health, with frequently hospital visits due to angina pain. His four bypasses were slowly blocking and he was told that he had only one more opportunity for surgery. In 1995, the best surgeon in Adelaide told him, "Mr. Pilling, I am sorry. I cannot operate because I believe I will kill you." David had to find a surgeon prepared to risk the operation to provide bypasses on his existing bypasses.

This serious threat to his health did not stop David from working. In the next month, he did a two-week seminar tour of New Zealand, a one-week engagement in Perth and a one-week management seminar in Queensland. In the meantime, Professor Buxton, who performed his original operation in Melbourne in 1982, examined him and said, "Well, we may as well operate because you are going to die anyway." David readily agreed.

In the meantime, David had been approached by the largest real estate group in Western Australia to come on board as their Managing Director, with the understanding that he could also continue his speaking career. With his typical optimism, he accepted the position and planned to commence after having the surgery. In April, 1995, Professor Buxton performed the surgery and successfully inserted three arterial bypasses. Two weeks after the operation, David, still wheelchair-bound, flew to Perth and commenced work against his doctor's orders.

The company had recently suffered losses of $250,000. Not only that, but there was very low morale among the franchisees. What they needed was direction and leadership, and David was able to provide both. Within one year, the business started to turn around, and within three years it had made a profit of $850,000. Whilst Perth is a beautiful city and a wonderful place to live, David preferred Adelaide, and he returned there in 1998. For the next two years, he ran the Western Australian operation while commuting between Adelaide and Perth.

In 2001, David launched his franchise operation 'Pilling Systems' which licensed offices to operate his real estate system featuring a unique set of selling techniques, quite different from those the industry employed. These techniques were called 'Buyer Ranged' and 'Set Sale'. During the ten years, he operated eighty-six offices using this system and wrote three more books on real estate. In June, 2011, with his health failing once more, he decided to retire from his real estate operations.

As a successful, self-educated man, David had a tremendous urge to share his learning with others and so, in his so-called retirement, wrote this book: 'Unlock the Giant Within'.

www.ingramcontent.com/pod-product-compliance
Lightning Source LLC
Chambersburg PA
CBHW022112170526
45157CB00004B/1604